Books in
General

Books in General
By Solomon Eagle

[First Series]
(JOHN COLLINGS SQUIRE)

Essay Index Reprint Series

 BOOKS FOR LIBRARIES PRESS
FREEPORT, NEW YORK

INTERNATIONAL STANDARD BOOK NUMBER:

0-8369-2136-4

LIBRARY OF CONGRESS CATALOG CARD NUMBER:

70-142699

PRINTED IN THE UNITED STATES OF AMERICA

ARTURO WAUGH

Preface

THESE papers are selections from a series contributed weekly, without intermission, to the *New Statesman* since April 1913. I do not feel that the responsibility for reprinting them rests on my shoulders; I trust that where it does rest it will rest lightly. I shall have done all I hope to do if I have produced the sort of book that one reads in, without tedium, for ten minutes before one goes to sleep.

The pseudonym " Solomon Eagle," I may explain, is not intended to posit any claim to unusual wisdom or abnormally keen sight. The original bearer of the name was a poor maniac who, during the Great Plague of London, used to run naked through the street, with a pan of coals of fire on his head, crying " Repent, repent."

S. E.

Contents

Contents

Who's Who

WORKS of reference are extremely useful; but they resemble Virgil's Hell in that they are easy things to get into and very difficult to escape from. Take the Encyclopædia. I imagine that my experience with it is universal. I have only to dip my toe into this tempting morass and down I am sucked, limbs, trunk and all, to remain embedded until sleep or a visitor comes to haul me out. A man will read things in the Encyclopædia that he would never dream of looking at elsewhere — things in which normally he does not take the faintest interest. One may take up a volume after lunch in order to discover the parentage of Thomas Nashe; but one does not put it down when one has satisfied one's curiosity. One turns over a few pages and becomes absorbed in the career of Napoleon. Thence one drifts to the article on Napier, which sends one to that on Logarithms in another volume; and when night closes in and (as we used to construe it) sleep brings rest to weary mortals, one still sits in one's chair, bending heavy-eyed over the book, with a dozen pressing duties left undone and the last post missed. By that time one has reached, perhaps, the abnormally complex diagrams which illustrate the article on Metaphysico-

13

Books in General

theologico-cosmolo-nigology — of which science, the reader will remember, Voltaire was the father and Herr Doktor Pangloss the first professor.

Who's Who takes me in the same way. Ordinarily I have no particular thirst for it. I should not dream of carrying it about in my waistcoat pocket for perusal on the Underground Railway. But once I have allowed myself to open it, I am a slave to it for hours. This has just happened to me with the new volume, upon which I have wasted a valuable afternoon. I began by looking up a man's address; I then read the compressed life-story of the gentleman next above him (a major-general), wondering, somewhat idly, whether they read of each other's performances and whether either of them resented the possession by the other of a similar, and unusual, surname. Then I was in the thick of it. There was nothing especially exciting about most of the information that met my eye. Generally speaking, the biographies were of people of whom I had never previously heard, and whose doubtlessly reputable achievements had been recorded in spheres as unfamiliar to me as the dark side of the moon. What can it mean to me that Mr. J. Fitztimmins Gubb worked for five years under Schmitt at Magdeburg and is now demonstrator in Comparative Obstetrics at the Robson Institute? Or that the Bishop of the Cocos Islands has been five times married and was educated at

14

Who's Who

King Edward VI Grammar School, Chipping Chester, and Pembroke College, Oxford? Yet I read of some six or seven hundred such, and found it as difficult to refrain from " Just one more " as would a wealthy dipsomaniac just parting from an old friend in a public-house at five minutes before closing time. I cannot easily account for the attraction. Something, I suppose, may be put down to the fact that character comes out in a man's account, however bald, of himself; and that the *Who's Who* autobiographies, in spite of their compression, exhibit many and diverse interesting traits of character. But mainly, I think, it must be that we most of us have collector's mania in some form or another, and that one cannot resist the temptation of collecting facts even when they are so irrelevant and of so little importance to one that they slip through one's fingers as soon as one has gathered them. For I am sure that I do not know now whether I have got the number of the Bishop's wives right, or the sites of his education, or even the name of his diocese.

I suppose that no one ever tells an untruth in *Who's Who*. There is not much scope for it, though it is conceivable that there may have been exaggerations of the truth. The compilers are extremely capable; and the contributors seem to be as uniform in their veracity as they are various in their loquacity. Only in rare circumstances could

15

Books in General

any one hope to impose on *Who's Who* without very rapid detection. An opportunity of that nature did once occur to me. There is a compilation called the *American Who's Who,* published (if I remember correctly) in Chicago. By some curious accident, which I have never been able to explain, its conductors got hold of my name — I don't mean " Eagle," but the other. By some accident more curious still they got the impression that I was an American settled in London; and with admirable enterprise they sent me, for two or three years in succession, yellow forms on which I was requested to inscribe my age, antecedents, and accomplishments. Each year I was dazzled by the idea of a joke which, I felt, would immensely amuse me, and which could (so the Devil argued) hurt nobody. On each occasion I filled the form exhaustively. I put down my name and address correctly; but beyond that not a word of truth did I tell. I invented for myself a career, a career not imposing enough to arouse suspicions, but far more picturesque than my actual career has been. I described my parents as being Homer E. —— and Anna P. ——, of St. Louis, Mo. I copied out of an American minor poet's autobiographical preface a list of academies at which I had been educated; and then I launched out.

I had, I stated, left America for Europe at the age of nineteen. I had written (I was cunning

Who's Who

enough to put down the names of one or two of my actual works) such and such books, including a Manual (for Schools) on Political Economy and a small brochure on Polycarp. I had travelled over four continents; my recreations were " all forms of sport, especially big-game hunting "; I had gone through the Balkan War as a volunteer with the Greek Army; and I possessed several decorations, including the Blue Boar of Rumania, the St. Miguel and All Angels of Portugal, and the fourth class of the Turkish Medjidie. Notice the fourth class; no common liar would have thought of so convincingly modest a claim as that. Each year, as I say, I lived laborious days in the delineation of an imaginary pedigree and a supposititious career. Then I broke down. There was no risk of punishment attached, and, I take it, small risk of discovery. But my softer self began telling me that it was a scandalous thing to hoax foreigners; that the trick was unworthy of an Englishman, or, indeed, an adult of any nationality, down to the most backward of Nicobar Islanders; and that the only fitting punishment for a person addicted to such practices would be to have pins put upon his chair by his children or his back chalked by infants in the street. I weakened and broke; sentiment overcame reason; my heart gained the victory over my head. And each year, with reluctant deliberation, I tore up the well-filled sheet and destroyed again my other self, my American self, the romantic self who had done

17

Books in General

the things I had never done, who had stalked the bear in the snowy fastnesses of the Caucasus and won the gratitude of exotic potentates. The forms have stopped coming now; but the memory of my vision still burns with a melancholy yet tender brightness; and those mythical progenitors, Homer E. —— and Anna P. ——, are to me all that his Dream Children were to Charles Lamb.

Political Songs

IF one goes up a mountain and surveys all the kingdoms of the world one sees a good many horrible things. Few of them are worse, in their way, than the modern political song. There have been bad political songs in all ages. Cæsar's soldiers used to sing some which were not merely uninspiring but irrelevant, and *Lilli Burlero* (or *Lillibulero*) itself was no great shakes as a poem although its tune had a swing. But there have never been any to equal in badness the kind of songs that has been generated by the British party system. The only modern politicians who ever manage to generate a good song are the Socialists. Socialist song-books, in spite of their plenitude of hack phrases about chains and freedom's dawn, always have a good deal of tolerable poetry in them. William Morris's political songs are excellent, and some of the modern foreign Socialist songs are really worthy expressions of the movement. When their words are not good their tunes are: witness the *Internationale* and that stirring Italian labour song that is now, I believe, prohibited by King Victor's Government. But the kind of songs that our good Liberals and Conservatives sing at their meetings are gruesome.

Books in General

I hold in my hand — as the saying goes — the *Liberal Song Sheet* now being used at big party meetings. One or two of the more facetious ditties show some ingenuity, and there is a certain go about the first line of "Stamp, stamp, stamp upon Protection"; but for the rest the only song the writer of which would not get a birching in any properly constituted society is Ebenezer Elliott's *God Save the People,* which is generations old. "Let who will make a nation's laws as long as I make its songs," said some writer. One might add: "Let who will make a nation's songs as long as they are not done by the people who make its laws." Caucus-provided laws may be all right, but caucus-provided songs, written by party agents and under-secretaries, are not successful.

The chief characteristic of the Liberal songs, apart from their metrical and linguistic peculiarities, is their insistence upon incongruous military image. Imagine Mr. Asquith donning bright armour and taking part in the incidents depicted in these verses — to the tune of *Who will o'er the Downs?*

> *Our leaders, tried and trusted men,*
> *   Still love the ancient faith,*
> *To Freedom and to Conscience true*
> *   In danger and in death.*
> *And they have donned their armour bright,*
> *   Their courage all aglow,*

Political Songs

To lead the toilers of the land
Against the Tory foe.

For years we've suffered pain and loss,
By privilege oppressed;
Our birthright has been filched from us
And left us sore distress'd.
But now our leaders — trusted, tried —
Are keen to strike a blow,
And wrest our stolen acres from
The proud, disdainful foe.

It is not my business to discuss the justness of
the judgments here implied, but what on earth is
the point of suggesting that Mr. Asquith, Mr.
George, Mr. Lulu Harcourt, Lord Haldane, and
so on, are true " in danger and in death "? They
may have come unscathed through the fire of Suffra-
gette dog-whips, but nobody calls them to die for
disestablishment. There is here an utter lack of
reality, a lack that must prevent these songs from
moving anybody to action, as good songs should do.
They are as conventionally false as the cheapest kind
of leading article.

Here are some more extracts from the same
source :

We defend the right we won in ages past;
We demand the measures by the Commons passed,
Let no Lords presume to wreck the work at last,

Books in General

For we go marching on.
Freedom for our trade and nation
From all insolent vexation,
For democracy's salvation
We all go marching on.

Peers and Tories may to wreck the work unite,
Britain's sons for Britain's freedom still shall fight;
None shall hinder us till triumph is in sight,
As we go marching on.

Then up to the sky with your Hip-hip-Hooray!
For the unbeaten leader, who leads us to-day,
For ASQUITH — *to-day, after long, weary years,*
Our victorious Captain o'er Tories and Peers.
Then cheer with a will for the great deed is done;
Attacking the Veto, we've fought and we've won;
Henceforward these islands of ours are to be
Not the Land of the Peers but the Land of the Free.

Long, long in shameful slavery
The emerald isle hath lain,
The victim of past knavery,
And Unionist disdain.
But Freedom's day is coming —
See how the foemen flee!
Home Rule is just
And come it must
To set old Ireland free!

Political Songs

One blow will end the matter!
Strike, strike it with a will!
The enemy we'll scatter
And quickly pass our Bill.
Our leaders are determined,
True followers are we,
Our arms are strong
To right the wrong
And set old Ireland free.

A curious thing is that almost universally in these songs the virtues and actions of the party leaders get almost as much attention as the political questions at issue. This is the mark of the caucus.

It is a very difficult thing to write a good propogandist song at all. A first-rate tune will often cover up the most prosaic words, but generally speaking political songs split on the rock of the specific. It is the greatest mistake to expect to stir people with verses dealing with a particular Bill. The spirit of freedom, the spirit of revolt, the passion of love, or the passion of hate, may make good songs, but it is a hopeless task to try to make poetry out of the taxation of land values or an import duty on corn. A good Socialist song may deal with brotherhood or service, but it cannot deal with " the nationalization of the means of production, distribution, or exchange." One should avoid the kind of concrete details that produce a sense of anti-climax,

23

and the kind of personalities that sound false. The spirit of Liberty may appropriately be depicted in a helmet, but it is silly to conjure up a picture of Mr. Asquith with a suit of armour over his frock-coat. Even the fact that a thing is glaringly true does not necessarily make it suitable for metrical statement. It is true that there is an insufficient supply of sanatoria and that the thought profoundly moves many people. But a song emphasizing the fact must be a failure. Modern political song-writers fail (1) because they are usually people who cannot write verse at all, (2) because they try to make their songs like extra-rhetorical speeches or articles. Probably the next Liberal song will deal with the ravages of pheasants.

An Oriental on Albert the Good

THE award of the Nobel Prize to Mr. Rabindranath Tagore is generally approved. I do not entirely agree with those who think that Mr. Tagore's poems are masterpieces in English; for I find his English poetical prose monotonous and without rhythmical beauty, although, in a sense, immaculate. But those who know the Indian originals say that they are really great, and that they have got a hold on the general population unprecedented for centuries past.

I have just acquired a book by an Indian poet who was not so wise in his choice of subjects as is Mr. Tagore. The book is an English version (made in 1864 by the tutor of Sir J. Jeejeebhoy's sons, and published by the Bombay Education Society) of an Epic on the Prince Consort by the Parsee poet " Munsookh." The poem is enlivening if not inspiring.

It opens with the usual Oriental invocation to Heaven, ending " With that remembrance alone will I fill the cup of my heart and sing new and entertaining stories." It then plunges straight *in medias res* with a first canto, " On the birth of Prince Albert, his education and arrival at mature years; and his wish to marry Victoria."

" There is a country of the world called Germany, the eminence of which is known everywhere. In its interior is a large district called the Dukedom of Gotha, about thirty-seven miles in area, and containing about one hundred and fifty thousand inhabitants. The air of this district is pleasant, dry, and cool; and the water refreshing and pure. The land is good and very fertile, and every article of food and clothing is cheap there. In its neighbourhood is the city of Coburg, where the richest blessings of Providence display themselves, near which flows the river Itz, and where is a magnificent ducal castle, having the appropriate name of Rosina, with a garden entirely surrounding it. Here the birth of Albert took place."

Prince Albert grew up wise and studious, and at last his preceptor said to him: " My accomplished pupil, this is the one hope of my soul, that thou make a hearty effort to be united to the worthy heiress of the Kingdom of England, and if thou do this, thou wilt not be disappointed. . . . Put in action therefore the effective dagger of contrivance; engraft speedily the plant of love . . . lose not thy time, for if thou do thou wilt be considered a fool."

Queen Victoria's portrait was sent to Albert, the

An Oriental on Albert the Good

bearer telling him that he was searching the world for a worthy, loving, and religious prince. "Thou hast administered the medicine for my secret pain," was the reply, and the Prince wrote a letter acknowledging the present. "When I would write thee a letter," he said, "the water of my eyes flows from my pen instead of the black ink. . . . In my feeling of love for thee I am mad: I am a moth flying around a candle. . . . Though I swim always in a flood of tears, my body is burning to a cinder." When Victoria's mother heard about this she was glad, but said that "the hearts of the English people are intoxicated with haughtiness; they despise a stranger and a foreigner . . . nor will they consider it honourable that thou should be united in love to a child of Germany." Various letters passed, but Albert's father was astonished at his rashness. "Foolish boy, heretofore engrossed in eating, drinking, and learning. Where didst thou get this information and these notions? . . . A nation proud and haughty like the English will think thee thoroughly mad." But letters from England convinced the Duke; he admonished his son as to his future behaviour; and the party sailed for the port of London, where "Victoria immediately went upon the terrace." The lovers met and sang, and the Prince returned home to complete his studies. "A little time after this occurrence the Queen again remembered Albert; she caused a letter, official, and according to rule, to be written to his father."

Books in General

" Albert's father prepared himself at once, taking necessary provisions, furniture, and money. Having sat in a boat Prince Albert went forward accompanied by his family. The gallant vessel floated down the stream, and did not leave her track on the way. From a distance she appeared like an alligator, or like the moon of the second day sailing through the heavens, or like a tree growing in the midst of deep waters, casting its shadows as it moved in a hundred directions; or she was like a horse leaping without feet, and bound only to the surface of the water, so swift and lofty of mien that the sun from afar uttered a shout of approbation. As a lover weeps on account of separation from his beloved, so the ship beating her breast, filled her skirts with water. She sometimes appeared from her motion tired and weary, and the bubbles about her seemed like blisters on the feet. In body she was a strong negress, but in speed lively; in her womb were hundreds of children, yet did she never bear."

" Albert thought the waves were like an infuriated elephant," but he arrived safely, and the marriage was celebrated amid general rejoicings.

" The voice of triumph arose from every side with guns and bells and bands of music; in every house, too, arose the heart-charming sounds of cornets, flutes, harps, pianos, and singing of various sorts; cannons boomed from every fort — one making a

28

An Oriental on Albert the Good

whirring noise, another a noise like thunder. . . .
So pure became the waters of the Thames that one
could see in them the image even of the soul of his
body. It was not a river, but as it were a flower
garden; and the bodies of the fishes glittered like
rose-leaves. Everywhere were clusters of variously
decked boats; the vessels were as shaking mountains,
which made graceful motions like peacocks coquet-
ting in the garden of Paradise."

A great banquet followed, and when "the reign
of wine" was finished the music began. "Trom-
bones sounded so impressively that letters were imprinted upon the face of the air." Then came the
dancing. "What shall I say of the Mendozas and
Polkas? for the philosophic and the pious lost their
peace of mind through them. . . . The Polka was
kept up with such zest and excitement that there was
a stir among the angels of heaven. . . . In short,
the ball was gracefulness itself which made the stars
bite their own bodies with jealousy." The dead rose
up from the ground enamoured of the dancing, and
the lamps put their hands over their eyes. The
festivities over the royal pair retired and sang to
each other.

Next year a princess was born, and all England
was merry. Other children followed, and for
twenty years the royal pair lived in happiness. In
1843 the Queen and the Prince revisited his native

29

Books in General

country in a ship furious as a leopard, that broke through hundreds of whales. Home awoke tender thoughts in the Prince. " Collecting himself he sang " a chant comparing himself to Joseph, and his bride to Zuleika — which indicates a somewhat different view of the Potiphar's wife episode from that prevalent in Occidental circles. The rest of the work is mainly taken up with the Great Exhibition, the Prince's death, and numerous maxims for the use of his son, such as :

" King must keep entirely aloof from several hurtful things as . . . chess.

" A king's country is like a beautiful woman, and the merchants of that country are, as it were, the precious jewels and ornaments of that woman; and the more these jewels and ornaments are, the more heart-charming and beautiful she looks."

This last aphorism is disputable.

Epigrams

ANY one who reads Mr. R. N. Lennard's charming little anthology of English epigrams in the Oxford Garlands Series will regret that the practice of writing poetical epigrams has died out. Until the Victorian age almost all professional writers, as well as many amateurs, tried their hands at epigram. If you had anything especially offensive to say about any one — and especially about politicians, doctors, and ladies unduly addicted to cosmetics — it was the natural thing to put it into a couplet or a quatrain. Ministers and Privy Councillors used to compose epigrams about each other; but who can imagine Sir Henry Dalziel writing witty quatrains about Sir Alfred Mond, or *vice versa*? Why the habit has died out I don't profess to say. There may be some significance in the fact that the great age of epigrams was the eighteenth century — the prose age *par excellence*. There is probably more in the decay of knowledge of Greek and Latin. When almost every educated man was familiar with the Greek Anthology and the works of Martial — whence all kinds of epigrams, elegiac, amatory, and satirical, descend — it was perhaps natural that the temptation to continue the good work should be generally felt. It may even be that

Books in General

a form so small is incapable of infinite variety and grows exhausted. Johnson wrote a ludicrous burlesque epigram —

> *If the man who turnips cries*
> *Cry not when his father dies,*
> *'Tis a proof that he had rather*
> *Have a turnip than his father.*

— and there is undoubtedly sound criticism in it. After a certain time the making of epigrams may proceed almost on a formula. At all events, the decline of the epigram is obvious. The well-meant effusions which the late Sir Wilfrid Lawson used to waft across the benches of the House of Commons were scarcely equal to the old level of our political quips; it is very rarely that a tolerable metrical epigram appears in the Press; and the poets have almost all abandoned the habit of attempting to get their thoughts into so small a compass. The custom of composing epigrams for private albums is virtually extinct. Every schoolgirl writes in every other schoolgirl's album that there is nothing Original in her excepting Original Sin; and even that not very splendid *mot* was constructed by Thomas Campbell nearly a hundred years ago. The rest is silence.

The greater number of our epigrams are satirical, and Mr. Lennard's selection is mainly composed of these verses with stings in their tails. One of

Epigrams

the most taking of these is A. Evans's on a Fat
Man:

When Tadlow walks the streets, the paviours cry
" God bless you, sir! " and lay their rammers by.

But that, perhaps, is not really stinging; if Mr.
Tadlow was good-tempered, he must have liked it
himself. Good couplets like these are few, but Coleridge's on the Swan-Song is one:

Swans sing before they die — 'twere no bad thing
Should certain persons die before they sing.

The most brutal epigrams we have are Byron's on
Castlereagh's suicide, after that statesman had cut
his throat. These are not very good, but Mr. Lennard gives them; and, in fact, almost every famous
epigram in the language. He classifies them under
headings: " Political," " Professional and Trading,"
" Amatory," and so on. Of the Literary epigrams
one of the best is Bishop Stubbs's on two of his nineteenth-century contemporaries:

Froude informs the Scottish youth
That parsons do not care for truth.
The Reverend Canon Kingsley cries
History is a pack of lies.

What cause for judgments so malign?
A brief reflection solves the mystery —

Books in General

Froude believes Kingsley a divine,
And Kingsley goes to Froude for history.

Lord Erskine's on Scott's Waterloo Poem is good:

> *On Waterloo's ensanguined plain*
> *Lie tens of thousands of the slain,*
> *But none, by sabre or by shot,*
> *Fell half so flat as Walter Scott.*

Theodore Hook's epigram suggesting that it would be impossible to find a reader who would pay for the binding of *Prometheus Unbound* now falls as flat as Scott, owing to the utter falsification of the prophecy.

Mr. Lennard gives a fair number of epitaphs, including Evans's well-known one on Vanbrugh and Gay's even better-known one on himself. But I don't think we have in English an epitaph so delightful as that written for his own tomb by the obscene French poet Piron:

> *Ci-gît Piron*
> *Qui ne fut rien,*
> *Pas même*
> *Académicien.*

Landor's " I strove with none, for none was worth my strife," however, could not be surpassed by any serious epitaph. From Landor Mr. Lennard has naturally had to draw freely for his more serious

34

Epigrams

sections. Landor came nearer than any English writers to rivalling the feats of the best Greek epigrammatists. Many people would say that his *Dirce* is the most beautiful epigram in the language.

Mr. Lennard's selection is, as I have said, a very good one. The only old one I miss is Richard Bentley's on German scholarship:

> *The Germans in Greek*
> *Are sadly to seek;*
> *Not one in five score,*
> *But ninety-nine more.*
> *All, all except Hermann —*
> *And Hermann's a German.*

The omission is the stranger in that Landor's greatly inferior epigram on Germans is included. About the longest poem admitted is Clough's revised version of the Ten Commandments: it is flat in places, but contains one famous couplet. Only when he comes to the moderns might Mr. Lennard have cast his net wider. Browning, who wrote some neat versicles, is unrepresented; and so is Mr. Watson, who, in his earlier days, wrote epigrams, some of which, if not masterpieces, were as good as some of Mr. Lennard's old ones. And it would have been worth while to collect a few of the miscellaneous modern ones that float about. There are Limericks — and some Limericks will satisfy the narrowest definition of an epigram — which would

35

be worth preserving; and then there are odd fragments like the effort alleged to have been written
on the blackboard by a Cheltenham schoolgirl:

Miss Buss and Miss Beale
Cupid's darts do not feel.
How different from us
Miss Beale and Miss Buss.

Tolerable modern epigrams are so few that it would
be worth while saving all there are.   Unfortunately
the pleasantest personal ones that one hears priv-
ately, though they would have been printed in a
franker day, must mostly remain unprinted in an
age when direct satire is considered ungentlemanly,
and the law of libel is so easily invoked.   I remember Mr. ——'s epigram on Lady —— and Mr.
——'s on Sir —— ——.   Mr. Lennard cannot be
expected to publish these.

An Eminent Baconian

A VERY curious chapter in the history of the Bacon-Shakespeare controversy closes with the death of Sir Edwin Durning-Lawrence. Amid all the strange multitude of retired judges, lawyers, astrologers, and American ladies who have championed the cause of Lord Verulam there has been no figure more singular than that of this affluent old ex-M.P., who, after a lifetime spent in business, platform speaking, and the study of modern mechanical improvements, suddenly plunged into the fight with unprecedented enthusiasm and methods of argument never equalled in their singularity. Setting out with the conviction that Shakespeare could not possibly have written the plays, and that Bacon was the only man who could have, Sir Edwin became so obsessed with the subject that he found proofs of his contention everywhere, and gradually came to the conclusion that Bacon wrote almost all the Elizabethan and Jacobean literature that is worth reading. We have heard of the devout mystic who sees " every common bush afire with God ": to Sir Edwin Durning-Lawrence every common bush was afire with Bacon. His outlook being of this character, it is scarcely to be wondered at that his meth-

Books in General

ods of reasoning and of research were most surprising. Most people who read his pamphlet, *The Shakespeare Myth,* must have been astounded by the *naïveté* of some of the " proofs " there contained. The fact that Bacon was called Bacon — a name so easily interchangeable with pig, hog, and rasher — was a great help; for where the application of ciphers did not obtain one word it might obtain another. Bacon, according to Sir Edwin, must have been at least as preoccupied with ensuring his identification by posterity as with the writing of good verse, for he would take great pains to work in such a word as " hang-hog," or to make three consecutive lines begin with words — such as Pompey, In, and Got — out of the initials of which could be constructed the appellation " pig." Everything was pork that came to Sir Edwin's net, and he would by tortuous ratiocination get evidence from the most seemingly innocent contemporary English and foreign engravings. For there was a secret brotherhood at work carrying on the Baconian tradition, and the artist who gave the portrait of Shakespeare two left sleeves (the confirmation of this was, I think, obtained from the editor of the *Tailor & Cutter*) had a subtle and profound intention. Sir Edwin collected a very large library in connexion with his work, and the study of it was his passion; but, save industry, he had none of the qualifications for his task.

38

An Eminent Baconian

I myself obtained in a strange way an amusing insight into his looseness of procedure. He had been writing letters maintaining his thesis in a contemporary weekly. Wondering whether he could be hoaxed, I sent to the paper a letter over what might have seemed, to a man with any real detective faculty, the suspicious signature " P. O. R. Ker." In this letter I called Sir Edwin's attention to a quotation (which I had myself invented and written in Elizabethanese) which I ascribed to one of the best-known works of Greene. My " quotation " (I forget its wording, but it contained phrases about " Shakescene " and " the semblance of a hogg ") made it perfectly clear that Shakespeare was merely Bacon's dummy. Any man with the slighest qualifications for his work would have looked up Greene for reference — and would not have found it. Not so Sir Edwin. He wrote in at once (the editor, in order to spare his feelings, did not print the communication) to say that the fact that Mr. Ker's important and convincing reference had been ignored by the Shakespeareans showed their utter incompetence.

But the most striking thing about him was his detestation of Shakespeare. There are people who hate Napoleon; there are people who object to Torquemada; there are even people who feel a pronounced distaste for Nero. But never has any one loathed and despised a dead man as the really

39

mild and amiable Sir Edwin despised and loathed Shakespeare. No epithets were, he felt, too opprobrious for this rascal, who for three hundred years had cheated another man out of his due fame. He denied Shakespeare any virtue at all; he pointed out that there existed no proof that Shakespeare could even read; and he habitually referred to him as the " drunken, illiterate clown of Stratford," " the sordid money-lender of Stratford," and " the mean, drunken, ignorant, and absolutely unlettered rustic of Stratford." So strong, indeed, were his feelings that when the *Times* says that " One cannot but feel that he was happy in not living to see the celebrations which the British Academy and other friends of literature are to hold in 1916, the third centenary of Shakespeare's — not Bacon's — death," it is not making a weak and untimely jest, but stating the sober truth.

Who will now take on Sir Edwin's mantle as the most conspicuous Baconian? Mr. George Greenwood is *hors concours* because, though an anti-Shakespearean, he has doubts about Bacon; and we have heard nothing lately about that romantic American doctor who a year or two ago began digging for evidence in the bed of the sylvan Wye. That another ardent combatant will soon appear is pretty certain; in fact, there will probably be a continual succession of such for all time unless — which is unlikely — somebody discovers documentary proofs

An Eminent Baconian

of Shakespeare's authorship so irrefutable that no one could dream of challenging them. For the examination of a mystery — if you can persuade yourself that there is a mystery — is always fascinating, and the search for and application of ciphers and hidden meanings produces such entertaining results that it would be almost worth while becoming a Baconian for the fun of it. Almost, but not quite.

The Beauties of Badness

THE collector of amusingly bad poetry has never had such splendid opportunities as to-day. The world is all before him where to choose. Modern cheap production has made it easy for any one who can raise £20 to get a volume of poems printed; and of recent years the field has been greatly enriched by the growing body of verse-writers in America and the Colonies. There have always, of course, been poets who have given unintentional rather than intentional pleasure. I have before me a volume published (at Cambridge) in 1825, entitled *Original Poems in the Moral, Heroic, Pathetic and other Styles, by a Traveller,* which contains poems in the following style — amongst others:

INGRATITUDE

My Muse, who oft recites on Love,
   Or Heavenly Beatitude,
Her strains more melancholy move
   Devoted to INGRATITUDE.

With thee, Dark Demon — what can charm?
   Nor manners polish'd — chaste, or rude;

The Beauties of Badness

Nor Friendship's hand — nor Safety's arm
So vile art thou — INGRATITUDE!

Tho' dear a Female's face, or form;
Tho' elegant her attitude;
We fly, as from the winged storm —
If she pours forth INGRATITUDE.

But it is seldom that the collector comes across one of these delightful relics from an older day. The greater part of any collection must be formed of books published within the last forty years. Our age may be — indeed, it is — deficient in some respects, but in the production of unintentionally amusing writers no age, not even the Renaissance or the great ages of Greece and Rome, can vie with it.

It might be possible for a man with the industry of a Herbert Spencer exhaustively to classify the writers of whom I am speaking, and to tabulate the qualities which give to their works their peculiar virtues — incongruity of image, unfortunate use of colloquialisms, hopeless slavery to the necessity of rhyme, and so on. I am no Spencer; indeed, the only things I have in common with that philosopher are a taste for billiards and the recollection of a single visit to the Derby. To me there is a single broad division which connoisseurs may find useful in arranging their collections: in one class we may put those poets who are specifically cranky; in the other those (some silly, some quite sensible people

43

Books in General

apart from their artistic proclivities) who (Macaulay's Robert Montgomery is the type) try to write poems like other people's, but whose total lack of poetic perception leads them into strange aberrations of expression.

The first kind are comparatively rare, but there are some good examples still going strong. There is, for instance, a gentleman (at one time a distinguished scholar of Balliol) who describes himself as " The Modern Homer," and has written a number of epics, including *The Human Epic, The Epic of London, the Epic of Charlemagne,* and *The Epic of God and the Devil.* Preoccupation with his matter leads him to such phrases as:

> *When Murder is on the* tapis
> *Then the Devil is happy.*

But he, perhaps, is not so interesting as Mr. William Nathan Stedman, who used to live in London, and now, I believe, is settled in Australia. This gentleman is addicted to prefaces proving that Mr. Gladstone, " this DIRTY OLD DEVIL," " this sly old wizard, a protoplasm from the abyss of nowhere," was the Beast of the Revelations, and he has an aversion from Mr. R. J. Campbell, whom he calls " moo-cow, kid-gloved Campbell." It is well worth while buying his *Sonnets, Lays and Lyrics.* The poems themselves are not so amusing, though we sometimes came across such ambiguous phrases as:

44

The Beauties of Badness

And when upon your dainty breast I lay
My wearied head — more soft than eiderdown.

But the illustrations — wood-blocks from eminent artists like Albert Dürer and Louis Wain — are charmingly irrelevant, and the prose passages are unique. The poet refers to the Laureateship —" an office I refused after Tennyson's death, though made with the offer of a premier's daughter and £30,000 " — and he is violently down on critics who have failed to see the merits of a certain novelist whom he calls " Queen Marie," " a woman who did you no wrong, nor envied ye your bones and offal, but gave Most Interesting Books for your betterment and education. Are ye not dirty dogs and devils? Eh? " " Bull-browed bastards " is one of the mildest terms he applies to the critics.

Difficult to place in either class are the poets who have some technical faculty, who are not necessarily cranks, but who endeavour to put such extraordinarily prosy things into verse that the result is as comic as though they were. I have, for example, a book containing " a lyrical romance in verse," which tells a story, that might have gone quite well in prose, of a man who falls in love with a girl and has long discussions with her about politics. The author's choice of a metrical form leads him to pages and pages of this sort of thing:

I ceased, and somewhat eagerly she asked:
" Then you would justify the Socialist,

45

Books in General

Or Anarchist, the brute assassin, masked
As a reformer, him who has dismissed
All scruples, and himself or others tasked
To murder innocence? Can there exist
A reason to excuse Luccheni's action,
Of life's great rights most dastardly in-
fraction?"

"Excuse it, no!" I said; "nor justify it;
But understand it yes! — I find confusion
In both your questions; and, your words imply
it,
They have their base in popular illusion.
In Socialism and Anarchism, deny it
Who will, there's no imperative inclusion
Of violence. Each, aiming at reform,
Would lay life's ever-raging life and
storm."

The growth of the Socialist and Suffragist move-
ments has led to a great increase in this kind of
argumentative verse; but the bad poems in the
Conservative or Militarist interests are generally
very much worse, a type-specimen being this:

And so with foes about us
Just waiting for their chance
We must become a nation armed
Like Germany and France.

Another example of Imperialist verse is:

The Beauties of Badness

I'm old John Bull of England,
My triumphs are in song.
I've fought and won great victories
Which did not take me long.

I've fought in many a battle
By sea as well as land.
I've fought in Russia, Belgium,
Africa and India's golden strand,

which occurs in a work appealing for better treatment for British Honduras.

But most of the best bad verse is not propagandist. Amongst the classics of the kind the Works of Johnston-Smith rank high. These have been published complete in one volume, but the best of them are to be found in a smaller book entitled *The Captain of the Dolphin.* Mr. Johnston-Smith had a great vocabulary and peculiar gifts of metaphor and of abrupt conclusion. Here are some typical passages :

A balminess the darkened hours had brought from
out the South,
Each breaker doffed its cap of white and shut its
blatant mouth.

Strike, strike your flag, Sidonia,
And lessen death and pain;
" Strike," " Fight " are but synonyma
For misery to Spain.

47

Books in General

On speedy wing the graceful sea-fowl follow fast —
They seem to me the souls of seamen drowned,
Who have for sailors, ships and ocean's briny blast
Dumb love which they are yearning to propound.

O'er the sea's edge the sun, a dazzling disc,
In splendour hangs, preparing for his plunge;
Upon the heaven's bright page he stamps an asterisk
Of yellow beams which Western things expunge.

Reluctant I leave, like a lover who goes
From the side of the maid of his choice,
By whom he is held with a cord actuose
Spun out of her beauty and voice.

" Actuose " is very characteristic of this poet, who uses enormous numbers of astonishing words of which he does not tell us the meaning, although he gives us a glossary containing such definitions as:

Derelict.   An abandoned ship.
Outward-bound.   Sailing from home.
Yo-heave-ho!   A phrase used by sailors when two
or more pull in concert at the same rope.

One of his nicest surprises is the ending of:

Where the sun circles round for the half of the year
And is cold — like a yellow balloon.

The kind of thrill produced by this unexpected end-

The Beauties of Badness

ing is, of course, common in verse. Some readers
will be acquainted with the epitaph:

> *Here beneath this stone at rest*
> *Lies the dear dog who loved us best.*
> *Within his heart was nothing mean,*
> *He seemed just like a human being.*

But a University poet's anticlimax on Actæon may
not be so generally known:

> *His hands were changed to feet, and he in short*
> *Became a stag. . . .*

Nor this affecting stanza from a woman's book recently published:

> *What o' the wind?*
> *It hisses through a vessel's spars.*
> *What o' the wind?*
> *It is in truth to mercy blind,*
> *It surely from all rest debars,*
> *And even frights the sturdy " tars."*
> *What o' the wind?*

An equal bathos is sometimes produced by inappro-
priate metaphor. The worst instance I know is
found in the poems of quite a well-known writer who
describes roses:

> *Aft before and fore behind*
> *Swung upon the summer wind.*

49

Books in General

But the author of a recent drama of the Near East came pretty near it with

> . . . *the diamond shaft of the fierce searchlight*
> *From the lens of the crystal moon.*

The chase after the unusual almost always means disaster. This is another recent example:

> *I have found thee, dear! on the edge of time,*
> *Just over the brink of the world of sense;*
> *In dream-life that's ours, when with love intense*
> *We function above, in a fairer clime.*
>
> *I have found thee there, in a world of rest,*
> *In the fair sweet gardens of sunlit bliss,*
> *Where the sibilant sound of an Angel's kiss*
> *Is the sanctioned seal of a Holy quest.*

But nothing produced in this manner is so attractive as the merely commonplace can be when carried to its farthest pitch. A year or two ago a young American published a volume with a preface ending: "He was apprised of the death of his invalid brother, whose remaining portion of his grandfather's legacy accruing to him facilitated the publication of this book." The epilogue ran as follows:

> *Oh, the rain, rain, rain!*
> *All the day it doth complain.*
> *On the window-pane, just near me,*

The Beauties of Badness

How it sputters, oh, how dreary!
One becomes so awful weary
With the rain, rain, rain.

The difference between this and Verlaine's *Il pleut sur la ville* would be hard to define, but there certainly is a marked difference.

Most of the poets quoted above have, at any rate, the gift of moving with some freedom within their metres. But some people who publish verse cannot even do that, however simple the forms they choose. They struggle through their poems like flies in treacle. A good example may be taken from a book (excellently produced) issued only a year ago by one of the foremost publishers. Apart from its other qualities, it shows a most extraordinarily revolutionary conception of the way in which lines may be ended:

A man's home is a woman's breast. There see
Him in infancy, and later, seeks he
Inspiration from the self-same source. 'Tis
His home, t'wards which, from cradle to the grave,
He doth gravitate, accomplishing his
Greatest works by aid of it. Man on the
Woman's aid depends. Oft unconsciously
'Tis given, oft loyally the truth's in
Loving breast safeguarded — less often 'tis
In cruelty withheld.

Books in General

This supplies the only case I know of in which the article " the " has been used as a rhyme. But for sheer struggle the poem does not excel parts of this other one, which was published in a recent anthology:

Along a marsh a hungry crane
With patient steps, his way did take
Each cranny of the rivage fain
To ransack with his slender beak,

When, suddenly, his watchful eye,
At but four paces distance, saw
A worm, that back, as suddenly,
To his subterranean hole did draw.

Nathless the crane did, straight, begin
His beak, and claw, alike, to ply
And hoping the retreat be, in
The end, of the insect might destroy,

The turf did tear up, and dispel
The clods, and with such vigour strive
That he, at last, perceives his bill
At of the cave the depth arrive;

But lo! just when of all his toil,
The object he was nigh to get,
Beneath his very nib, a mole,
Without ado, devoured it!

Thus often, lurchers, onward who
Are prone by shady ways to creep

The Beauties of Badness

*May the reward to those that's due
Who, openly, have acted, reap.*

This fable is called by the author *A Surreptitious Catch;* but it might equally fitly have been entitled *The Apotheosis of the Comma.*

I have, as I say, insufficient scientific talent to enter upon an analytic criticism of this kind of poetry; and in this brief discourse I have done little more than string quotations together. But that operation is all that is needed to serve my present object — viz. the propagation of the cult. Any one who has ever read the novel of Mrs. Amanda M'Kittrick Ros knows how much sustenance the human spirit may derive from the byways of literature; but it is very rarely that one meets, even amongst the best-read of men, one who is conscious of the peculiar poetic treasures that lie about in the publishers' offices and on the second-hand bookstalls simply imploring to be collected.

More Badness

MY appeal for interesting specimens of bad verse has brought me a large mass of material; but most of my correspondents seem not to realize that merely feeble and meaningless verse is so common as not to be worth preserving. The best single line I have received — sent me by a notorious dramatist who has forgotten its place of origin —is:

The beetle booms adown the glooms and bumps
among the clumps;

and what promised to be the best whole poem is one that begins by rhyming " Atlantic " to " blanket." But when I had got through it I found that my correspondent had got it out of a visitors' book in an hotel. I really cannot count anything that has not been properly published; although I confess to being tempted by such lines as:

Farewell, farewell, bonny St. Ives,
May I live to see you again,
Your air preserves people's lives
And you have so little rain.

More Badness

So really the best acquisition I have made is the following, the author of which I should like to discover:

In this imperfect, gloomy scene
Of complicated ill,
How rarely is a day serene,
The throbbing bosom still!
Will not a beauteous landscape bright
Or music's soothing sound,
Console the heart, afford delight,
And throw sweet peace around?
They may; but never comfort lend
Like an accomplished female friend!

With such a friend the social hour
In sweetest pleasure glides;
There is, in female charms a power
Which lastingly abides;
The fragrance of the blushing rose,
Its tints and splendid hue,
Will, with the seasons, decompose,
And pass as flitting dew;
On firmer ties his joys depend
Who has a faithful female friend!

As orbs revolve, and years recede,
And seasons onward roll,
The fancy may on beauties feed
With discontented soul;

Books in General

A thousand objects bright and fair
May for a moment shine,
Yet many a sigh and many a tear
But mark their swift decline;
While lasting joys the man attend
Who has a polished female friend!

My correspondent says that he received this from a friend (perhaps a polished female friend), who did not tell him whence it was extracted. I myself have seen two lines of it before — the last two of the second stanza. They occurred in a letter I received some time ago from a clerical acquaintance who was apologizing for having got engaged. He, on inquiry, pretended (with a mendacity very rare amongst clergymen) that he had written the lines himself; but I did not believe him. The poem bears the marks of the earlier decades of the nineteenth century. Can it be by Thomas Haynes Bayly?

One interesting thing I should like to trace is a metrical version of Holy Writ containing such lines as these on Jonah:

Three dreadful days beneath the deep,
In fish's belly dark lay he.
How terrible methinks his fate.
May no such torment fall on me.

The most ingenious writer who contributes the " Observator " column to the *Observer* offers me a couple

More Badness

of specimens, one of which is new to me. The old one is the late Mr. Alfred Austin's remark about Nature:

> *She sins upon a larger scale*
> *Because she is herself more large.*

And the other, a touching narrative of a gipsy woman who fell ill, was a discovery of Andrew Lang's:

> *There we leave her,*
> *There we leave her,*
> *Far from where her swarthy kindred roam,*
> *In the Scarlet Fever,*
> *Scarlet Fever,*
> *Scarlet Fever Convalescent Home.*

A Mystery Solved

APPARENTLY the poem about " a polished female friend " is to be found in one of Mr. E. V. Lucas's books. It was written, it seems, by a parson named Whur or Whurr, who flourished in Norfolk about a century ago. Whur delighted in all calamities, and described a father, on the birth of a child with no arms, exclaiming: " This armless child will ruin me." No one has yet brought to my notice any whole volumes of bad verse worth acquiring, though various choice fragments have reached me. There is an epithalamium ending:

> *And never, never she'll forget*
> *The happy, happy day,*
> *When in the church, before God's priest,*
> *She gave herself away.*

There is an *in memoriam* poem beginning:

> *Dear Friends, we had a sudden Blast*
> *Which came to us unexpected.*

And there is a loyal song to their present Majesties in which occur the lines:

A Mystery Solved

Our King and Queen are never proud
They mingle with the densest crowd.

But the most attractive new specimen is a poem on
the late monarch's death.   It was printed and sold
as a broadsheet in London, and runs:

> *The will of God we must obey.*
> *Dreadful — our King taken away!*
> *The greatest friend of the nation,*
> *Mighty monarch and protection!*

> *Heavenly Father, help in sorrow*
> *Queen Mother, and them to follow,*
> *What to do without him who has gone!*
> *Pray help! help! and do lead us on.*

> *Greatest sorrow England ever had*
> *When death took away our Dear Dad;*
> *A king was he from head to sole,*
> *Loved by his people one and all.*

> *His mighty work for the Nation,*
> *Making peace and strengthening union —*
> *Always at it since on the throne:*
> *Saved the country more than billion.*

There are two more verses.   Personally, I find this
considerably more interesting than any of Mr. Alfred Noyes's various Coronation Odes.

Carrying the Alliance too far

WHY is it that Japanese authors are allowed to write in English newspapers any sort of barbarous jargon they like? Mr. Yoshio Markino was the first to be licensed. To start with, one found his " delightfully quaint " English amusing in a mild way, but with repetition his sedulously cherished howlers became irritating. Still, he was only one; and primarily a painter at that. But now Mr. Yone Noguchi has turned up, and he is doing the same thing. Mr. Noguchi is considered in Japan — at least so his friends tell us — the first poet of the day. Those who remembered his last residence here assured us that on his return he would compel all men — like Helen of Troy or Mr. Tagore. He comes. One is prepared to be conquered. One turns to one's *Westminster Gazette* to read his works; and one finds there columns of stuff, possibly inspired, but certainly written in such pidgin-English that one cannot bother to read it.

Mr. Noguchi's pidgin-English is not of quite so curious a breed as Mr. Markino's, but it is sufficiently bad. One does not blame him for that.

Carrying the Alliance too far

He writes English a great deal better than I do Japanese. But why on earth cannot the newspapers who print his works translate them into normal English? Is it that their sub-editors shrink from the task? Is it that they fondly believe that we are all so fascinated by English of the Noguchi-Markinesque brand that we had much rather have it than any other sort; or is it that a tradition has been established that Anglo-Japanese articles are not to be altered? If this is true, it is a thousand pities that, for all their charm, Mr. Markino's early productions were not unmercifully damned. What should we say if newspapers began printing in all their native crudity articles by Frenchmen and Germans imperfectly acquainted with the tongue of this country? Suppose some journal came out next week with an essay beginning:

" What sadly fall the leaves of automne! What of sadness tumble on the heart because that the winter put his snows on all the country. And sad also the spring, the spring who arouse the love in the soul, and who make to think to all the springs of the time past. My heart weep like a bird who have lose her companion."

Or suppose a German were allowed by the *Westminster* to present its readers with a political article opening:

Books in General

"No Dutcher has the by Mr. Gamaliel Zoop, Amerikansh postaltelegrafkommunikationdepartment minister on politishekonomy famose lecture to a at Manchester people-coming-together delivered recently without outerorderly pleasure read."

Obviously we should not tolerate it. Can it be that, even after the war with Russia, even after Japanese professors have written works on sociology, the superstition lingers here that a thing cannot possibly be truly Japanese unless it has the odour of an old curiosity shop?

None of this, I may say, is meant to be discourteous to Mr. Noguchi. I merely suggest that it would be better for him if he vetoed every endeavour to print his English articles as he writes them. If he were the Japanese Homer — indeed, he may be that for all I know — I should say precisely the same thing. Can he be aware that even his faulty spelling goes uncorrected?

May 1914

I WRITE " these lines " just after arriving in Berlin. Not that I have anything to say about that. I merely mention the fact. It may explain my difficulties. The journey is really very dull. All those hundreds of miles over the Great Plain of Europe with never a hill except the ridge of Minden, very little water, nothing but endless flat fields sprinkled with trees, church spires, and red farm-houses. There is simply nothing to look at. If you put your head out of the window at Osnabrück, you may see some coal; and at Münster you may, if you choose, speculate as to which of the people on the platform are Anabaptists. That is not much during a twelve-hour run from Flushing.

A pleasant travelling companion is an alleviation on such occasions. The other occupant of my carriage had points about her. She was a young, cheerful, and rather obese Jewess going home with a plethora of scarves and wraps, several boxes, two lobsters (for her father), and a canary. At Goch she was incensed to find that she had to pay a heavy duty on the lobsters, so heavy that it would have paid her better to get the creatures in Berlin and have a drink on the balance. This story might make an

63

Books in General

illustration for one of Mr. Lloyd George's homely speeches on Free Trade. But there was no duty on the canary. In his little cage, covered with a green curtain, the canary sat, non-dutiable but very phlegmatic. At frequent intervals his mistress lifted the green curtain, looked him in the eyes with a bewitching smile, and piped " Peep, Peep." The bird never replied, though perhaps he looked his response. The lady then turned to me and said, " Is 'e not a nice bird? Is 'e not goot? " and common politeness — leaving gallantry out of the question — compelled me to reply always, " Yes, a beautiful little bird." About twice an hour she retired to the dining-car and came back exuding smiles and sighs " I half joost 'ad a bifsteck. I dawn't like steck." How true it is that in life we have to be content with second-bests! But I did not discuss the matter.

In intervals of silence I finished Mrs. Russell Barrington's *Life of Walter Bagehot* (Longmans, 12s. 6d. net). It is a strange thing — and unfortunate, since so much material has disappeared with the passage of time — that Bagehot should have had to wait nearly forty years for a biography. But now it has come it is an interesting one. The author being Bagehot's sister-in-law (daughter of James Wilson, who founded the *Economist*), the work has rather a family air. Bagehot's more obvious virtues are a little too much insisted upon, and excessive

64

importance is attributed to irrelevant details. The long description of his ancestry and birthplace, for instance, might have been curtailed. But the *Life* is well written; it contains a great many interesting letters, and it gives a really living picture of one whom Lord Bryce has called " the most original mind of his generation."

One would wish, however, for a supplement giving a fuller analysis of Bagehot's literary work. Mrs. Barrington gives little more than a list of the titles of his essays. It is true that to most people Bagehot is still primarily the political and economic writer. There are few intelligent Englishmen to-day who have not been influenced by *The English Constitution* and, in a lesser degree, by *Physics and Politics*. His *Economic Studies* make the rudiments of political economy as simple and even as entertaining as a good fairy-tale, and those who have read *Lombard Street* speak of it as a masterpiece. But the most extraordinary thing about it is that this man, who knew all about currency, who was in the confidence of Chancellors of the Exchequer, and who invented Treasury Bills, was also one of the most illuminating and sympathetic literary critics that England has ever produced. Personally I find his literary essays inferior to those of no other English critic who was not himself a poet, and I think that in some respects, though not in all, they are better than Arnold's.

Books in General

Probably Bagehot's celebrity as an economist militated for some years after his death against the popularity of his literary work. Many literary people, looking through the complete list of his works, and seeing *Literary and Biographical Studies* jostling shoulders with works on money, may very pardonably have assumed that these Studies, however able, must have been of a dry, hard character. They are very far from that; no English criticism is more human than his, less coldly intellectual; his temperament, naturally emotional and mystical, was most valuably reinforced by the balance, the tolerance, the sanity that were developed by his more mundane activities, but the temporal man in him never overcame the eternal. Such essays as those on Hartley Coleridge, on Shelley, on Dickens, on Cowper, on the *Edinburgh* Reviewers, are bound before long to be recognized as among the great classics of English criticism. Naturally he was not impeccable; posterity may think, for example, that he attached too much importance to his friend Clough. But he is usually completely convincing. Take the following passage from the comparison of Wordsworth and Jeffrey:

" A clear, precise, discriminating intellect shrinks at once from the symbolic, the unfounded, the indefinite. The misfortune is that mysticism is true. There certainly are kinds of truths, borne in as it were instinctively on the human intellect, most

May 1914

influential on the character and the heart, yet hardly
capable of stringent statement, difficult to limit by
an elaborate definition. Their course is shadowy;
the mind seems rather to have seen than to see them,
more to feel after than definitely apprehend them.
They commonly involve an infinite element which, of
course, cannot be stated precisely, or else a first
principle — an original tendency of our intellectual
constitution, which it is impossible not to feel, and
yet which it is hard to extricate in terms and words.
Of this latter kind is what has been called the religion of Nature, or more exactly, perhaps, the religion
of the imagination. This is an interpretation of the
world. Accordingly, to it the beauty of the universe
has a meaning, its grandeur a soul, and its sublimity
an expression. As we gaze on the faces of those
whom we love; as we watch the light of life in the
dawning of their eyes, and the play of their features,
and the wildness of their animation; as we trace in
changing lineaments a varying sign; as a charm and
a thrill seem to run along the tone of a voice, to
haunt the mind with a mere word; as a tone seems
to roar in the ear; as a trembling fancy hears words
that are unspoken; so in Nature the mystical sense
finds a motion in the mountain, and a power in the
waves, and a meaning in the long white line of the
shore, and a thought in the blue of heaven, and a
gushing soul in the buoyant light, an unbounded
being in the vast void of air, and

Books in General

Wakeful watching in the pointed stars

" There is a philosophy in this which might be explained, if explaining were to our purpose. It might be advanced that there are original sources of expression in the essential grandeur and sublimity of Nature, of an analogous though fainter kind to those familiar, inexplicable signs by which we trace in the very face and outward lineaments of man the existence and working of the mind within. But be this as it may, it is certain that Mr. Wordsworth preached this kind of religion and that Lord Jeffrey did not believe a word of it."

The visionary and the epigrammatist are near allied, and both the practical and the ideal in Bagehot are illustrated in his own phrase: " If you would vanquish Earth, you must invent Heaven." Bagehot, as he appeared to ordinary people every day, is portrayed in another sentence. " He left many," it is said, " with the idea that he was a good fellow, yet with no idea that he was a great man." A great man can have no better epitaph.

May 1914: The Leipzig Exhibition

ANY one who imagines that the English can, or at all events do, compete with the Germans in beauty of book-production had better go to Leipzig this summer and visit the Buchgewerbe und Graphik Exhibition — or " Bugra," as it is universally called in Germany. The new railway station — the finest in the world — is also worth going to see; but that, presumably, will last after this year. In many respects the exhibition is like all other big exhibitions. It is much too enormous to be capable of thorough inspection. Leaving out of account the huge buildings devoted to the mechanics of printing and so on, there are a palace (" The Hall of *Kultur,*" of course), filled with engravings and photographs; a colossal structure containing the exhibits of German publishers of books and music; and pavilions for most of the other nations of the earth. Even Corea has a building — though I did not see it — and Siam is well to the fore. The exhibition grounds are very extensive; they contain (need I say?) a " Street of Nations," many fountains, and countless cafés. There is a reproduction of Heidelberg Castle, full of drinking-cups and the

Books in General

weapons with which German students put a little interest into each other's faces. There is a Bavarian Hall, where real peasant maidens bring your beer and the latest and cheapest musical-comedy tunes are played by real peasant musicians, with feathered hats and costume complete down to the bare knees that they insist on retaining in the face of a proclamation by the local Catholic hierarchs to the effect that such a display of naked charms is grossly indecent. There is no wiggle-woggle, but there is a waterchute and a shooting-gallery whose proprietors invite you to come in and try your skill at " live objects." The man who was with me — he is a person who, like Mr. Galsworthy, would not touch a fly " save " (as the old verse has it) " in the way of kindness,"— refused to come in. Naïvely distrustful of aliens he was afraid, he said, that the targets might be dogs. But he need not have been alarmed, for we were afterwards informed that they were merely big game thrown on a screen by a cinematograph. When you hit an animal it did not drop, but a red light showed.

Naturally comparisons between the exhibits should be made very cautiously; the exhibition is being held on German soil and the German display is much larger than any other. In many respects England shows up very well. The English section in the *Halle der Kultur* is certainly as good as any, and the etchings shown by Mr. Muirhead Bone, Mr.

70

May 1914: The Leipzig Exhibition

Charles Shannon, Sir Charles Holroyd, and other British artists are possibly the very best things in the place. The main English exhibit is housed in a pleasant Tudor building with some beautiful rooms. The Shakespeare exhibit of editions and portraits is most interesting for those who like that sort of thing; a fine collection of original Beardsley drawings has been lent by Mr. Lane; the Caxtons are coming; there are admirable specimens of the works of the Kelmscott, Riccardi, Florence, and other presses; there is a gallery of Medici prints unsurpassed by any colour-reproductions in the exhibition (the print of the Dresden Van Eyck triptych is the most completely satisfying colour-print I have ever seen); and the elaborate bindings by Riviere's, the Oxford Press, and other establishments are not inferior even to the exquisite leather bindings by Noulhac and R. Kieffer shown in the French building. Everything our officials could have done has been done to perfection; and the special exhibits have been very well chosen. Where we fall sadly short is in the ordinary book of commerce.

I cannot but think that the English publishers who have taken stalls — and, of course, the selection of exhibits here had to be left to the publishers themselves — could have brought together a more attractive-looking lot of books than they have done. Most of them — I mention no names — seem to have bundled together their books without any consideration either of the contents or of the appearance of the volumes. Of course there are English publishers who have no fine books and few decent-looking books on their lists; but some of the specimens at Leipzig look almost like remnants which it is hoped to sell off to visitors. But even if all the English publishers had shown all their best books, and none of their worst, they would still have been put in the shade by the Germans. Even the French publishers — whose achievements in typography and in illustration have been great — are not now fit to be mentioned in the same breath as the Germans.

The German exhibits are a revelation. The mid-Victorian tradition in print and design — which was so tenacious in Germany — has now been almost completely abandoned. I don't suggest that all German books are more presentable than English ones. Scientific works, theology, and shilling fiction are equally ugly in both countries. But there are today in Berlin, Leipzig, and Munich at least a dozen firms publishing for the ordinary market books whose average of beauty is far higher than that reached by the books of any considerable English publishing firm. Many thousands of really beautiful new books are now being produced every year in Germany; and of what can be done, especially in the way of making cheap books look presentable, our own publishers have no idea. There is, of course, a much larger educated reading public in

May 1914: The Leipzig Exhibition

Germany than in England. In every bookshop you are confronted by volumes of Dehmel, Hofmannsthal, and other writers who, were they Englishmen, would never reach large circles of readers in their lifetimes. Anthologies of contemporary German poets sell literally by tens of thousands; and you can even get an infinite variety of doses of classical and modern authors by dropping pennies into automatic machines on the stations. This much may be admitted: that there is a larger literary public and more interest in contemporary art, literary and pictorial. But, even granting all that, the German publishers in meeting the market have shown a taste, and above all an enterprise (sometimes reaching audacity, no doubt), which most of our own publishers have never revealed in the slightest degree.

To give a full account of the show is beyond my ability, desire, and space. But in looking at the latest products of commercial colour-printing in the French pavilion I was struck by the extraordinary divorce between craftsmanship and taste in modern industry. Here were some of the vilest pictures (I don't mean morally) ever moulded by the mind of man; yet the experts were raving over them as being the last word in their own kind of colour-process. Needless to say, the exhibition, not being half over, is not yet completely ready. The Italian pavilion, when I was at the exhibition, could not be entered at all, and there were other lacunæ all over the place.

Books in General

This is the kind of thing that makes the whole world kin.

Amongst the German authors whose portraits grace the walls of the exhibition is Mr. George Bernard Shaw. They have naturalized him, like Shakespeare, and the next thing will certainly be a statue at Weimar.

The Mantle of Sir Edwin

I HAVE just spent three days reading Mr. E. G. Harman's *Edmund Spenser and the Impersonations of Francis Bacon,* published by the firm of Constable. There are books which he who runs may read; there are also books from which he who reads will run. This to me comes into neither category. It is very large and crowded with most complicated detail; it is, though quite competently written, devoid of literary grace; and it supports a monstrous thesis with arguments many of which are of staggering absurdity. Yet in point of deadly fascination it vies with the basilisk. It is a monument of the " scientific method." The author's learning and industry are terrifying; his tone seems completely dispassionate; he proceeds from discovery to discovery with mild ruthlessness; and not the most uncompromising of Wospolus was ever more sternly resolved to embrace logical conclusions. His chief fault is that his premises are usually arbitrary or quite insufficient; but the objective charm of his massive progress, as of a steam-roller, from stage to stage, is not affected by this.

Mr. Harman does not in this volume discuss in detail Bacon's authorship of Shakespeare's plays.

75

Books in General

He assumes that. He assumes also that Bacon did publish literature under the rose and that he did employ impersonators; his reasons being that he had to express his feelings and that acknowledgement of authorship would have damaged his prospects of political promotion. This much granted, Mr. Harman looks around for writings in which he thinks he can detect traces of Bacon and examines the evidence for their reputed authorships. He does not descend to the puerile level of the late Sir Edwin Durning-Lawrence, with his " Hic, Hæc, Hog." He says nothing of cryptogram. But in case after case he finds (1) that there are marks of Baconian thought and language, (2) that allegorical references to Bacon's political disappointments may be found, (3) that documentary evidence supporting accepted authorships is very slight. Nothing stops him. Where there is a real resemblance in style things are easy. Where there are marked differences we are asked to note the fact that Bacon's method enabled him to write in a variety of styles — as though serious writers expressing their inmost selves could put on styles like trousers. If somebody has borne witness that an Elizabethan wrote his own works, then that somebody was in the plot too.

As to Spenser, with whom Mr. Harman chiefly deals, one is certainly struck with the paucity of the evidence for him. We know less about him than we know about Shakespeare; and his biographers have

The Mantle of Sir Edwin

had to rely almost entirely upon "internal evidence" drawn from his works. But personally I must say that I prefer their methods to Mr. Harman's. He, analysing exhaustively the plot of the *Faerie Queene,* with its Britomarts, Arthegalls, and Blatant Beasts, finds a knowledge of court life that could not be possessed by Spenser, who lived in Ireland and was (according to him) an ex-Board School boy in a small Civil Service job — which is at any rate politer than "drunken, illiterate clown." This is question-begging; but what shall we say of the assumption that if Spenser had written the poem the rivers of Ireland would have been described as fully as the rivers of England? Why should the emigrant Civil servant know anything about the rivers of Ireland? As far as that goes, there is one slip in the description of the rivers of England which indicates to my mind that the author relied on some inaccurate map for his information about them. The Baconian authorship forces Mr. Harman to the conclusion that some of Spenser's sonnets were written by Bacon when he was eight or nine years old. But Mr. Harman is a strong man. After all, Mozart was a precocious child, so why not Bacon? He does not shrink from this any more than he shrinks from arguing that any book or letter which favourably mentions one of Bacon's cryptic works must also have been written or instigated by him. They *must* have been written by him, and, this granted, internal corroboration must be sought for. Anything is good enough for this purpose. Mr. Harman even finds evidence in the occurrence in several " Baconian " works of the phrase " golden wyres " as applied to the Queen's hair. If he would read the body of Elizabethan lyrics, or even extracts of them in such a contemporary anthology as *England's Parnassus*, he would find that an Elizabethan poet could no more help comparing a lady's Hayre to Golden Wyres than he could help likening her Teares to Pearles or her Brests to Iuorie.

But there is no space here for detailed examination. It is enough to yield oneself to the pleasure of following the Harmanian trail. I have noted the works which in the course of his narrative or in footnotes he ascribes to Bacon. The Authorized Version of the Bible is not mentioned. But, apart from his voluminous acknowledged writings, Bacon wrote the works of Spenser (including the *Faerie Queene*, the longest poem in the world, which Bacon published before he was out of his twenties) ; the works of Shakespeare; practically the whole body of Elizabethan poetical criticism (including Webbe's *Discourse of Poesie*, Puttenham's *Art of Poesie*, Sidney's *Apologie*, Daniel's *A Defence of Ryme*, and Meres's *Palladis Tamia*) ; many of the poems of Gascoigne (written by Bacon before he was twelve) ; certain works imputed to Nashe, Greene, and Gabriel Harvey; the poems of Sir Walter Raleigh and the *Last Fight of the "Revenge"*; the works of

78

The Mantle of Sir Edwin

Essex; Sidney's *Arcadia* and *Astrophel and Stella* (with this key Bacon unlocked his heart); Lyly's *Euphues* (a long book); Bryskett's *Discourse of Civil Life;* Sir Humphrey Gilbert's *Discourses* and the account of his last voyage; *Leicester's Commonwealth* and *Leicester's Ghost;* and other minor scraps. If this be all correct, we shall have to revise our opinion of the Elizabethan time as a time replete with various genius. All we shall be able to refer to now will be " the spacious Bacon of great Elizabeth."

An enormous number of people — including supposed writers and their relations — must have been in the secret. Sometimes they must have marvelled at Bacon's extraordinary behaviour, as for instance when he wrote for Raleigh a laudatory poem on the Queen:

" Bacon (who, in my opinion, is the author of the poem) makes use of the opportunity in taking up the personality of Ralegh to express his own feelings. He was undoubtedly most unhappy at his exclusion from access and the waning of all his hopes of advancement. This is what is reflected under the disguise of Ralegh's loss of favour in the poem."

They must have wondered how on earth Bacon expected his grievances to be remedied if his complaints were published over another man's name, and why, if Raleigh could address poems to the Queen *in propria persona* without loss of caste, Bacon could not do the same. But no doubt most of them, for many were impecunious, did not allow such questions to bother them much. They were content to take Bacon's bribes for the use of their names. What he must have spent in subsidies to sham authors one gasps to contemplate. No wonder that for years he was in such financial straits, and that at one point things came to such a pass with him that he was arrested for debt.

"The Cattle of the Boyne"

I HAVE referred before to the frequency of misprints in the penny *Times*. It does seem a pity that the conductors of the paper cannot keep it up to its old traditions in this respect. Last week there was a more curious instance than usual. These words appeared:

" The anniversary of the Cattle of the Boyne was celebrated with unusual enthusiasm throughout Canada."

I was so moved by the report of these zoological novelties that I made a little poem about them, full of Celtic twilight. It runs thus:

THE SANDS OF BOYNE

Och, Geoffrey, go and call the Cattle home,
  And call the Cattle home,
  And call the Cattle home,
    Acrost the sands of Boyne.
Shure, ye're the bhoy that's got inured to foam,
    So come, bring in the koine.

Och, are they fish, flesh, fowl or good red herrings?
  Perhaps they are red herrings,

Books in General

Forlorn and wildered herrings,
Strayed from their native broine,
This hapless party which has lost its bearings
Fornint the sands of Boyne.

No, no, they have no herring for their father.
The proof-reader's their father,
A most prolific father
By mishap or desoign.
If this is what wan penny means, I'd rather
Stump up the ancient coin

Than daily find — Och tempora, Och Times! —
Bad grammar in my Times
And misprints in my Times
In ivry other loine,
Capped by this worst of typographic crimes
" The CATTLE *of the Boyne"!*

But perhaps one ought not really to complain of misprints, even in the *Times*, when they are funny.

August 1914

AND it is less than three months since I was writing complacently about the Leipzig book exhibition! I wrote about the exquisite collections of bindings and drawings, the bands, the parading crowds of peaceful Germans, the pavilions of all nations from Holland to Siam, and the charming Tudor structure erected by Britain, with its long low halls containing cases of Shakespeare folios and editions from the Kelmscott Press. Enormous crowds from all over Europe would, it was hoped, visit the exhibition as the summer wore on. " August, of course," said the officials to me, " will be *the* month."

The buildings in the wide Street of Nations are still there, no doubt. The flags, perhaps, have been hauled down, but those files of white wood and plaster palaces still stand behind their flower-beds along the broad avenues. The crowds are dispersed. The officials in charge of the various buildings have fled to their respective domiciles. The cheerful male members of the Bavarian Peasants' Band have taken off their green hats and put on helmets, left the women behind, and gone off to burn villages like their own, and disembowel sunburnt French peasants as naturally amiable as themselves. Memories so recent make the pit of one's stomach sink. In May last a German barber in Berlin had his razor at my throat, and when he scratched my skin he was most concerned and apologetic. " Nescis, mi fili, quam parva sapientia regitur mundus." The remark was made by a Swedish statesman in the eighteenth century. Voltaire, looking down from heaven — if one may risk his displeasure by presuming his presence in so uncongenial a place — must feel that since the eighteenth century there has been no great change, and that the human race is as horribly ridiculous an institution as ever it was.

But here we are.* Like most other inhabitants of the " civilized " world, I have for the last week read no books, but only newspapers. Fourteen a day is about my average, which means nearly a hundred a week. And nine-tenths of them contain nothing that one did not know before. There never was a war, since telegraphs were invented, about which news was so scarce. Almost every rumour that comes through is dubious, and it is invariably contradicted. In successive issues and even in the same issue of a journal one reads that troops have and have not entered a certain village, that somebody's neutrality has and has not been violated, and

* I have left all this as I wrote it.— S. E.

that a naval engagement has and has not taken place. If you go over the eight pages of " war news " in a daily and make a summary of the unquestionable facts contained therein, as distinguished from the doubtful reports and the office-written padding, you find it could all be got into a paragraph. We have frequently heard that the day of the war correspondent was over. We heard it during the Russo-Japanese War — of which we certainly got very little news — and we heard it during the Balkan campaign. But at the moment of writing I have scarcely seen a single item regarding a single encounter which looked indisputable or which appeared to come direct from an eye-witness. Almost all the information we have been getting has come either from rumour travelling across many tongues or from official sources. Both these founts of news are great liars, the former excelling in the *suggestio falsi,* and the latter both in that and in the *suppressio veri.*

The desperate straits in which we have been for news could be gathered (if in no other way) from the outlandish places of origin ascribed to reports that get into print. Stockholm informs one that advices from Teheran report a conflict at Toul; and we hear that the *Mercure de Bruxelles* states " on excellent authority " that something has happened at Basle. Deliberate fabrication has been at work all over the place. Our good old friend the doctor, with the cholera microbes which he puts into wells,

Books in General

even turned up at the very start. This mythical
gentleman is at least as old as the Franco-German
War of 1870, and his last appearance was in the
Balkans. No sooner does a war start than one of
the combatants hastens to describe his diabolical activities in the hope, presumably, of making the
world's blood boil at the thought of an " outrage
against humanity."

The papers cannot be blamed for printing rumours, but they might give the clearest indication,
whenever possible, of the value of their sources.
Rumours before they get into print presumably travel
in much the same way as after they get into print.
Of how rapidly " news " develops I had an experience in a club on Tuesday night. A late evening
paper printed a brief report, stating that Aberdeen
doctors had gone to attend to wounded who were
being landed at Cromarty. Five minutes after I
had seen this, I was told by a member that single
British and German destroyers had had a brush off
the Scottish coast. Five minutes after that the vessels had expanded into flotillas, and within the hour
a club servant, with very gloomy face, remarked to
me, " I don't know if you've heard it, sir, but
there's been a great naval battle in the North Sea
and the British Fleet has met with an awful disaster." With correspondents kept out of the area
of hostilities, it is no wonder that by the time reports
of occurrences reach the persons who send them to

our newspapers they bear very little relation to the events (if any) which have originally generated them. War correspondents in Europe to-day seem to be able to do little more than sit in friendly foreign capitals and send home little bits of news out of the local papers. And if we want a really accurate and full description of the big battles, especially the big naval battles, of the future we shall usually have to wait until peace allows combatants to publish such books as the Japanese *Human Bullets,* describing the attack on Port Arthur, and those vivid Russian books which told the story of Rozhdestvensky's voyage to the China Sea with his mouldy squadron and the magnificent and pitiful end of it at Tsushima. But of no great modern war will the whole truth ever be properly known. Forces work over such vast areas that full information is impossible to collect.

Mrs. Barclay sees it through

OVER *the turmoil of a world in arms*
There floats a rich indomitable coo . . .
'Tis Barclay. . . . Though excursions and
alarms
Torture the firmament, though Wilhelm II
In shining armour waits his Waterloo,
Though on all sides the blood rains down in torrents
Love's interests still are in safe hands with Florence.

What though the rest of us are turning tail,
    Assured by those who have a right to speak
That only Patriotism has a sale?
    She knows Love's drawing-power remains unique;
    Her books need never be postponed a week;
Sure of her subject, certain of her vogue,
She has no need to adjourn, much less prorogue.

Business as usual.   Yet who knows, who knows
    Whether she has not chosen the better part,
Swelling the proud full sail of her great prose
    Still with the gentler zephyrs of the heart,
    Rather than seize an Amazonian dart,
Leaping into the middle of the fray
Like certain other poets of the day.

Mrs. Barclay sees it through

Has Robert Bridges' success with fighting
  Been such as to encourage emulation?
Or Dr. Watson's " bit them in the Bight "-ing?
  Or the same author's other lucubration
  (Yet one more blow for a disthressful nation)
In which, dead gravelled for a rhyme for " Ireland,"
He struggled out with " motherland and sireland "?

Did even the voice from Rudyard Kipling's shelf
  Say anything it had not said before?
And was not Stephen Phillips just himself?
  And was not Newbolt's effort on the war
  Distinctly less effective than of yore?
And would not German shrapnel in the leg be
Less lacerating than the verse of Begbie?

When the Muse seized me, in this manner, by
the hair, it was three o'clock in the morning, and
I had just finished the new novel by the author
of *The Rosary*. Had it been earlier I should have
written more. But next day the mouse of inspiration had fled to its hole; the spell of the book had
been dissipated; my vision had faded into the light
of common day; and I resumed my consideration of
the position of Przemysl, a place of which, until
this week, I had never heard. But what a fascination the book exercised while one was reading it!
I can well understand why Mrs. Barclay commands
a greater audience than perhaps any other living
writer. She can beat the basilisk at its own game.

Books in General

The reader is swept away with a rush of strong emotion at the very start. A tall, reticent, bronzed man arrives by the boat train at Charing Cross. Thrown over by a woman, he has been abroad for ten years, nursing his grief and creating a reputation as a novelist. No sooner does he get to the station than he extracts from the coy bookstall clerk a confession that to him the books of Rodney Steele are the best in the world. Lump in the throat number one; and a sovereign in the pocket of the clerk. Steele leaves the station to drive to a flat a friend has left him. Oh, the fragrance and glitter of dear old smoky London! Oh, the beauty of the Queen Victoria Memorial!

" Mysterious through the gloom, he saw the nation's fine memorial to a deathless memory. The gush of green waters, the golden figure at the summit, needed sunlight for their better seeing. But clear through the orange darkness gleamed the white marble majesty of England's Great Queen.

" Rodney Steele lifted his hand in reverent salute as he passed. . . .

" ' Lest we forget! ' quoted Rodney Steele as he looked at the majestic marble figure, throned outside the palace above the rushing waters. ' Yet — could we, who really remember, ever forget? ' "

The rest of the book tells how he was wooed and won by his old love, now a widow. She had

Mrs. Barclay sees it through

deserted him under a misapprehension and was resolved to recover him. She therefore took the next flat to his — or rather to her brother's, which Steele was occupying. She had heard that owing to a change of telephone numbers her brother was constantly being rung up by mistake for a Hospital. One night therefore Steele was rung up and a Kind Voice asked for the Matron. The voice reminded him of Madge. He began to feel so lonely that he willed, with all his will, that the unknown Kind Voice should ring him up again.

" ' Speak to me again,' he said, ' you, you spoke to me last night. Speak to me again. What wait I for? I wait for you! Just now — in my utter loneliness, in my empty solitude — I wait for you.' . . .

" The distant clock slowly chimed a quarter past the hour of ten; and — as that sound died away — the bell of the telephone rang."

This time he made the Kind Voice promise to ring him up nightly in order to console him in his loneliness. The Kind Voice consented. Ultimately on the telephone they discussed (he not revealing his identity or knowing hers) his novels. This is the kind of thing they say over the telephone:

" ' The thing of first importance is to uplift your readers; to raise their ideals; to leave them with a

Books in General

sense of hopefulness, which shall arouse within them a brave optimism such as inspired Browning's oft-quoted noble lines.' "

When finally he confesses to the Kind Voice that his life has been ruined by a girl with whom he is still in love, Madge thinks the time ripe for an appointment. They meet. He finds that the Kind Voice has been Madge all the time and he steels his breast against the woman who has added deception to her previous crime. But her " gracious gracefulness " and other qualities win in the end, and we finish at Christmas with Herald Angels and wedding-bells.

Mrs. Barclay certainly has skill. Nobody else can write a silly story half so well as she. Her English is fluent and vivid, although loose; her humour is genuine if not subtle; and she handles her dialogue, such as it is, very cleverly. But, above all, she knows how to serve out the glamour and the pathos with a ladle. The hero of this book is as generous as he is clever. He can conjure; he can make seagulls settle on his shoulder; and he does kind actions to widows. There are also an heroic ex-soldier who saved a man's life at Spion Kop; a bishop's window brimming over with love and reminiscences; and an honest, stupid Englishman with no thoughts of self. The only bad character dies, and the end is a pæan of joy. As long as she can keep

Mrs. Barclay sees it through

this up Mrs. Barclay will never lose her hold. In spite of the war, this book, I should think, will sell in millions and millions.

Vorwärts reports that Dr. Ludwig Frank, a member of the Reichstag, has been killed in battle near Lunéville. Dr. Frank, who sat for Mannheim, was one of the leaders of the Southern Revisionists. I had tea with him at the Reichstag last May. He took me into the Strangers' Gallery of the House, where I heard Dr. Liebknecht makes one of his anti-armament speeches, the one in which he incidentally accused a Prussian general of negotiating sales of decorations. It seems very remote now. Dr. Frank was barrister; a big Jew with a heavy, handsome face — sallow skin, aquiline nose, black moustache, strong chin, dominating eyes. His romantic air — he was supposed to resemble Lassalle — made him very popular in the rich Jewish salons of Berlin. He was a strong man, and one would have said an ambitious one. But a middle-class man who enters the German Socialist Party sacrifices so much that he *ipso facto* clears himself of the suspicion of mere ambition.

A Topic of Standing Interest

THE Oxford University Press has just issued a beautiful little edition of Erasmus's *Praise of Folly,* with a good reproduction of Quentin Matsys' portrait of Erasmus as a frontispiece. The last edition of the *Encomium Moriæ* with which I am familiar is that issued in 1887 by the firm of Hamilton, Adams. It had a binding which did not please, but contained Holbein's interesting illustrations. Whether any considerable sale of the book is likely nowadays I very much doubt. Erasmus's humour was an improvement on mediæval humour, which, except in a few cases, cannot make a modern man laugh save sometimes through the brazenness of its indecency. Erasmus was a child of the Renaissance, a wit, a scholar, a questioner of all things, a man of the world, a revolutionary conformist. But there are long dull passages in his most famous book, and many remarks that seemed most daring to the men of his own time are to us platitudinous; whilst he often labours some obvious joke in the worst mediæval way.

At the same time, any one who cares to go through the book will find occasional amusement. Erasmus

A Topic of Standing Interest

had a mild theory of the satirist's rights. "Wits,"
said he, "have always been allowed this privilege,
that they might be smart upon any transactions of
life, if so be their liberty did not extend to railing";
and he disclaimed a desire to imitate Juvenal by
"raking into the sink of vices to procure a laughter."
With these qualifications, he let out all around him
with some vigour. The personification of Folly is
rather feebly sustained, though the character is pleas-
antly introduced with the sentence: "I was born
neither in the floating Delos nor on the frothy sea,
nor in any of the privacies where too forward moth-
ers are wont to retire for undiscovered delivery."
But the *obiter dicta* on various classes of men who
have often been the butts of satirists since his day
are still entertaining and must in his own time have
been shocking. He refers to priests as "wisely fore-
seeing that the people, like cows, which never give
down their milk so well as when they are gently
stroked, would part with less if they knew more,
their bounty proceeding only from a mistake of
charity." He speaks of "The Carthusians, which
order alone keeps honesty and piety among them,
but really keeps them so close that nobody ever yet
could see them," and he is especially down on the
scholastic theologians. Sterne, it will be remembered, described a dispute "as to whether God could
make a nose as big as the steeple of Strasburg."
This is scarcely a caricature of the kind of discussion
ridiculed by Erasmus:

95

Books in General

" Whether this proposition is possible to be true; that the first person of the Trinity hated the second?

" Whether God, who took our nature upon him in the form of a man, could as well have become a woman, a devil, a beast, an herb, or a stone. And were it possible that the Godhead had appeared in the shape of an inanimate substance, how he then should have preached his gospel? Or how have been nailed to the cross? Whether if St. Peter had celebrated the eucharist at the same time our Saviour was hanging on the cross, the consecrated bread would have been transubstantiated into the same body that remained on the tree?"

Word-spinning he detested, and he refers the Nominalists, the Realists, the Thomists, the Albertists, the Scotists, etc., to the primitive disciples who were " well acquainted with the Virgin Mary, yet none of them undertook to prove that she was preserved immaculate from original sin."

" The disciples baptized all nations, and yet never taught what was the formal, material, efficient, and final cause of baptism, and certainly never dreamt of distinguishing between a delible and an indelible character in this sacrament."

Chaucer, with his observations about relics and " pigges bones," and the novelists who never hesitated to put friars in the most ignominious positions

A Topic of Standing Interest

(e. g. in chimneys and under tables) had made sport of the clergy, but Erasmus's particular method of battering current theology had not been so devastatingly employed since Lucian. He showed, like Rabelais, that it is possible to reconcile the profession of Christianity with something of what a recent writer calls " the old Voltairean love of humanity."

Erasmus made the familiar sport of lawyers and pedantic critics. He would have agreed with Sterne: " Of all the cants which are canted in this canting world — though the cant of hypocrites may be the worst — the cant of crticism is the most tormenting." " When any of them," he says,

" has found out who was the mother of Anchises, or has lighted upon some old unusual word, such as bubsequa, bovinator, manticulator, or other like obsolete cramp terms, or can, after a great deal of poring, spell out the inscription of some battered monument: Lord! what joy, what triumph, what congratulating their success, as if they had conquered Africa, or taken Babylon the Great! "

It was for such people's benefit that he must have made his irritating final remark: " I hate a hearer that will carry anything away with him."

Erasmus was the mildest of the famous satirists, but he has his place in the great succession, though

Books in General

his works cannot now compete for readableness with those of Lucian, Rabelais, Swift, Sterne, and Voltaire. Satirists have usually been considerable plagiarists, and *The Praise of Folly* has an important historical place in the development of this kind of literature. Richard Burton cribbed a good deal from it, in spite of his own drastic remark about persons who " lard their lean bookes with fat of others' workes " and his question: " If that severe doom of Synesius be true it is a greater offence to steal dead men's labours than their cloaths, what shall become of most writers? " But Burton has an account on the other side, for Sterne later on reprinted chunks of his work almost literally without any acknowledgement whatever.

The new Oxford edition gives a modernized reprint of the Caroline Version by John Wilson. In the introduction Mrs. P. S. Allen gives some interesting bibliographical particulars. Over forty editions of the *Encomium Moriæ* were published in the author's lifetime; within forty years of its first Latin issue French, Italian, and English translations had been published; and later versions have appeared in (amongst other languages) Swedish, Czech, Polish, and Modern Greek.

Was Cromwell an Alligator?

SOME people — who at least avoid the error of ascribing the invention to Steele or Addison — say that Abraham Cowley was the Father of the English Essay. It might alternatively be suggested that Q. Horatius Flaccus was one of its parents and Montaigne the other; Bacon having, so to speak, a watching brief at the birth. But the other statement is true in a sense: for though in patches Bacon (and Burton) anticipated the tone and method of that type of writing which was brought to its fullest perfection by Charles Lamb, Cowley was the man who fixed the type. His essays have just been republished in a beautiful little edition of the Collected Prose Works, issued by the Oxford University Press, and edited by Mr. A. B. Gough. Mr. Gough is a most painstaking editor, and his notes are abnormally full. They are so full that one feels that most people who are likely to acquire such a book will find nine-tenths of them unnecessary; but one ought not to grumble at that, since they have the complementary advantage of always supplying information when one looks for it.

The edition is especially to be welcomed as there are many persons capable of appreciating Cowley who have never come into contact with him. " Who now reads Cowley? " Pope asked in 1737; if the question were repeated to-day you certainly would not get a forest of hands raised, even in an audience replete with pince-nez and bulging brows. It was Cowley's misfortune, as it was his ambition, to be known in his own days as one of the greatest poets of his time; when men discovered that he was not that, they at once concluded that he was nothing else. Not that his poems are as negligible as some critics assert; his mere skill and neatness make him worth reading. Even if he had, as Mr. Gough remarks, " too little passion and spontaneity to be a great lyric poet," he was at any rate a good metrist and a most admirable phrasemaker. But his prose writings are certainly superior to the others; and this is true not only of the Essays. His *Vision Concerning Oliver Cromwell,* for example, is full of witty and whimsical things. Occasionally he employs very drastic language, as when he refers to the Protector as an " alligator " and when he abuses him for meditating the calling in of the Jews. This is how Cowley disports himself. The italics are mine:

" From which he was rebuked by the universal outcry of the Divines, and even of the Citizens too, *who took it ill that a considerable number at least among themselves were not thought Jews enough by their own Herod.* And for this design, they say, he invented . . . to sell St. Pauls to them

for a synagogue, if their purses and devotions could
have reacht to the purchase. And this indeed if he
had done onely to reward that Nation which had
given the first noble example of crucifying their
King, *it might have had some appearance of gratitude,* but he did it onely for love of their Mammon;
and would have sold afterwards for as much more
St. Peters (even at his own Westminster) to the
Turks for a Mosquito [Mosque]. Such was his
extraordinary Piety to God, that he desired he might
be worshipped in all manners, excepting only that
heathenish way of the Common Prayer Book."

But this strong language is not the strong language
of a man whose breast is a burning fiery furnace; it
is the invective of a man who is amused by his opponents and who regards them chiefly as pegs for
cunning sentences. His hard words would certainly
have broken no bones; and one can even imagine
that, in the secrecy of their chambers, the Puritans
themselves — at all events, the less ironsided of
them — may have shaken their sides over his char-
acter-sketch of the man whom they doubtless referred to in public as " our great leader."

But if such qualities are defects when a man is
writing political tracts or attempting the higher
flights of poetry, they are invaluable to him if he is
writing essays. Cowley's Essays — and his Prefaces are as good — are most delightful, and they
have as personal a turn as Lamb's. They all, vir-

Books in General

tually, have one text: the Sabine Farm text; the retired *Urbs in Rure* text. They speak of the country's charms in the ex-townsman's way; they gibe at the turmoil and press of cities in a manner which attests a still lively interest in these contemptible things; they praise the pleasures of horticulture, solitary meditation, and à Kempis's " little book in a corner." Their learning is lightly worn; their language natural; their arguments not so serious as to stand in the way of any jest that offers itself; and many passages in them might almost as well have been written in 1720 or 1820 as in 1660. These, for instance:

" There is no saying shocks me so much as that which I hear often that a man does not know how to pass his Time. 'Twould have been but ill spoken by Methusalem in the nine hundred sixty ninth year of his Life.

" I have been drawn twice or thrice by company to go to Bedlam, and have seen others very much delighted with the fantastical extravagancie of so many various madnesses, which upon me wrought so contrary an effect, that I always returned, not only melancholy, but e'en sick with the sight. My compassion there was perhaps too tender, for I meet a thousand Madmen abroad, without any perturbation; though, to weigh the matter justly, the total loss of Reason is less deplorable than the total depravation of it.

Was Cromwell an Alligator

" I thought when I went first to dwell in the country, that without doubt I should have met there with the simplicity of the old Poetical Golden Age: I thought to have found no inhabitants there, but such as the Shepherds of Sir Phil. Sydney in Arcadia, or of Monsieur d'Urfé upon the Banks of Lignon; and began to consider with myself, which way I might recommend no less to Posterity the Happiness and Innocence of the Men of Chertsea; but to confess the truth, I perceived quickly, by infallible demonstrations, that I was still in Old England.

" The civilest, methinks, of all Nations, are those whom we account the most barbarous. There is some moderation and good Nature in the Toupinamhaltians who eat no men but their Enemies, whilst we learned and polite and Christian Europeans, like as many Pikes or Sharks prey upon everything we can swallow."

The last sentence reads, perhaps, more like a certain living writer than like, say, Charles Lamb.

The best of Cowley's Essays are *Of My Self* and *Of Greatness*. I have no room to quote them at length. The first — in which he is writing of poetry and of his childhood's memories — is more full of feeling than is usual with him. The other is one of the most picturesque pieces of light moralizing in the language, full of what we all call the Playful Irony of the Gentle Elia, as in sentences

Books in General

like: " The Ancient Roman Emperours, who had the
Riches of the whole world for their Revenue, had
wherewithal to live (one would have thought) pretty
well at ease, and to have been exempt from the pres-
sures of extream Poverty "; and it describes the
pleasures of littleness most alluringly.   But some-
how, in spite of his assertions, one never quite believes in the genuineness of his middle-aged prefer-
ence for " Prettiness," as against " Majestical
Beauty."   One suspects the existence in him of a
disappointed ambition, a hankering after action,
which frequently afflict men who are constitutionally
fitted for nothing but looking on and making charming comments.   But he had certainly been very
badly treated by the Stuart family, which he had
faithfully served.   The Restoration gave him
neither employment nor money.   It gave him, however, a very fine funeral.   Evelyn says that his coffin
was followed to the Abbey by a hundred noblemen's
coaches and large numbers of wits, bishops, and
clergymen.

The Depressed Philanthropist

I DO not see why any one but myself should be interested in the mere fact that, except in the way of casual reference, I have always avoided writing a line about Mr. John Galsworthy. But as one's feelings commonly typify those of some section or other of one's fellows it may be relevant to one's purpose. I frequently begin writing something about Mr. Galsworthy and then tear it up. I constantly feel like abusing him, and am then checked by the thought that after all he is too good a man to go for. He is a sensitive and humane man of very great intelligence. He is a conscientious writer and an acute observer. He has a great respect for truth and a desire to state it at all costs. He detests pettinesses, hypocrisies, and shams. On almost every issue that might arise I am sure I should find myself voting on the same side as he, though perhaps we might differ in our views of the relative importance to be attached to the problem of World Peace and that of the hardships inflicted by mandkind on ants, wasps, and bees. And yet as I read his books I feel as if I were in some cheerless seaside lodging-house on a wet day.

I have just been reading his new miscellany *The Little Man*. The book does not show his qualities

Books in General

at their best, but it shows his defects at their worst. The principal contents are *The Little Man* and *Studies in Extravagance*. The first is a short play showing how a German, an American full of altruistic platitudes, and two self-contained and " proper " English people shrink in the most selfish and cowardly way from a forlorn baby suspected (falsely, of course, for the sake of the extra irony) of typhus. The " studies " are examinations of various " types " such as " The Artist," " The Plain Man," " The Housewife," " The Preceptor," and " The Latest Thing." And there is none of them good — no, not one. Mr. Max Beerbohm once did a cartoon of Mr. Galsworthy Looking upon Life and Finding it Foul, Life being represented as a fat and ferocious goblin with horns, a forked tail, and teeth like a wild boar's. It was just a little wrong. Mr. Galsworthy's vision should not have had so much of the positive about it. He does not find Life vigorously diabolical, but meanly cruel and pallidly contemptible. Many great men have been gloomy or pessimistic. Mr. Hardy is not exactly a merry grig, Schopenhauer was consistenly disgruntled, and the man who would look for *joie de vivre* in Leopardi would look in vain. And as Mr. Galsworthy suggests himself — it is a commonplace — it is often the duty of a serious contemporary writer to be horrifying, unpleasant, and shocking. The regeneration of mankind — to continue the commonplace — is not possible if we hold the view

The Depressed Philanthropist

that things may be done that may not be discussed, and that the failings of man and the diseases of society should, as far as possible, be stowed away in the cupboard, where the skeletons are. What is wrong with Mr. Galsworthy is that one cannot quite believe him. One suspects him of cooking the evidence. One does not mind a man presenting a black view of life if (*a*) he is temperamentally inclined to it and can be melancholy with a certain gusto, or (*b*) if, being a professed realist, he appears to have taken cognizance of every aspect that has presented itself to him. But Mr. Galsworthy presents so one-sided a case that we at once suspect his *bona fides* and react against his views. It would be unfair to classify him with that school of novelists who give their books titles like *Dull Monotony* and live up to their titles by giving a photographic reproduction of an intolerable tedium peculiar to, and comprehensible by, the households which they themselves afflict. He usually escapes being thoroughly boring partly because of his gift for occasionally happy and incisive phrase and partly because here and there, behind the grey brow of the dejected Hanging Judge, one catches a gleam of something more exhilarating than his expressed sentiments. But he is often very nearly dull, all the same: for his realism is often bogus. He starts with an intention to paint a caricature in greys, and a caricature which is not amusing. Even in his very well-made plays the characters are not, to my mind, usually interesting in themselves. One does not believe in them as persons. They are just a set of types, as stagy and unreal as the old stage figures of melodrama, though they are called charwomen, clerks, magistrates, and company directors instead of being called Irishmen, highwaymen, and wicked baronets. His plays argue cases, but they do not present life as we know it. I find the same sort of unreality about his prose; and, since the unreality takes the form of making mankind look utterly paltry and uninteresting, one wonders why on earth a man who has such an opinion of it bothers about it at all.

So in *The Little Man* and in these studies. All these average people do not get a dog's chance; we have all sinned and fall short of the glory of God, but we really are not quite so dull, feeble, and silly as all this. Some characteristics — as those of the Plain Man — are very cleverly recorded, but the whole of the man is not here, nor even the most important parts of him. As an illustration of Mr. Galsworthy's pseudo-realistic method take him on the ground most favourable to him — that of the beef-and-whisky-fed sportsman:

" What led to him was anything that ministered to the coatings of the stomach and the thickness of the skin . . . to be 'hard' was his ambition, and he moved through life hitting things, especially

108

The Depressed Philanthropist

balls — whether they reposed on little inverted tubs of sand or moved swiftly towards him, he almost always hit them, and told people how he did it afterwards. He hit things, too, at a distance, through a tube, with a certain noise. . . ."

Now, apart from the fact that a full and accurate description of a sportsman would put in many things Mr. Galsworthy leaves out (e. g. some indication that he was a human being, as we know the species), this is not good, though it is superficially plausible description, even so far as it goes. The plain statement that the gentleman played golf and cricket and shot a good deal would convey a better idea of him than this specious circumlocution. To say that a man is smoking a cigarette positively contains a greater measure of suggestion than to say that he is inhaling grey fumes through a cylinder of paper filled with dried herbs. Much of Mr. Galsworthy's attack upon all kinds of men and women, self-centred authors, idealists who oppress their wives, worldly women who have never found their souls, cultured people who chase the new, and Philistines who run away from the new, has the same sort of defect. It is really " guying " which passes for photography merely because it is heavy-footed and unamusing. I object to Mr. Galsworthy's ostensible view of life partly because I don't believe he takes it, and partly because if he did I should think it an absurdly unjust view. At heart a humanitarian, he has got into a dismal and costive kind of literary method which makes him look like a fretful and dyspeptic man who curls his discontented nostrils at life as though it were an unpleasing smell. As Ibsen used so often to remark, there is a great deal wrong with the drains; but after all there are other parts of the edifice.

A Polyphloisboisterous Critic

I REMEMBER — that is to say, I wish I remembered, for I have forgotten most of it — a poem that I used to recite at my mother's knee. Its subject was an antediluvian man of sesquipedalian height, who let out the blood of an ichthyosaurus with a polyphloisboisterous shout; and its claim to attention was a plethora of polysyllables very embarrassing to an infant, and indeed to any, tongue. It was of that poem that I was reminded whilst reading *European Dramatists*, by Archibald Henderson.

Mr. Henderson, an American professor, is not a stranger to the British public. It was he who produced, a few years ago, a biographical study of Mr. Bernard Shaw so vast that a single copy might well have served — were not Mr. Shaw still happily with us — as Mr. Shaw's tombstone. The work, indeed (to use the phrase Mr. Henderson himself applies to a play of Strindberg's), was " colossal in its incommensurability." It was the kind of book one had thought could only be produced by a large committee of Chinese scholars; and although it did not lead one to respect the author's powers of judging the relative importance of his various facts, it at

Books in General

least compelled one to admire his colossal energy and his incommensurable supply of these facts. From *European Dramatists* one gets precisely the same feeling. Parts of the book have appeared in journals published in Boston and in Berlin, in Stuttgart and in Stockholm, in Helsingfors, Paris, New York, and Ghent. And one may be sure that Mr. Henderson could have talked to the editors of all these papers and beaten all of them hollow in knowledge of the modern literature of their respective countries. The actual subjects of his papers are familiar enough: Strindberg, Ibsen, Shaw, Maeterlinck, Granville Barker, and Wilde. But in discussing them he shows an amazing acquaintance with everybody who has recently written anything in any country. He can refer you to the December 1913 issue of the *Przemysl Review*; he can tell you what the Servian critic, Ivan Peckitch, thinks of the Finnish poet, D. D. Bilius. He knows all about everything, though one is not quite sure that he knows anything else. But what chiefly pleases one about him is not so much what he says as the charming way he says it. Like Hudibras, he cannot ope his mouth but out there flies a trope. Everything happens with him in metaphors; people are always digging into soils, moulding things in fires or clothing them in vestures. And above all he is polysyllabic and rotund of speech.

He begins well with Strindberg, of whose first

A Polyphloisboisterous Critic

married years he observes that they " were undoubtedly happy — certainly in the passional sense, if not
in the restful consciousness of hallowed union."
" In 1886," he proceeds, " Strindberg began to be
obsessed with the monomania of animadversion
against the female sex." Later, " goaded by titanic
ambition, he cast off the shackles of provinciality for
the freedom of cosmopolitanism "— i. e. he travelled. Ibsen and Strindberg were " so antipodal in
temperament, yet so cognate in the faculties of in-
tuitive perception and searching introspectiveness."
One of Strindberg's works blurs the vision of the
average spectator, " with its kinetoscopic hetero-
geneity of spiritual films ": Peer Gynt (on the other
hand, shall I say?) stood for " the disciplinary bankruptcy of laxity." " Concretizes " and " inscena-
tion " are the kind of words he rejoices in, but perhaps two or three longer extracts will better illustrate the quality of his style:

" To peep into the workshop of the great master's
brain and assist at the precise balancing of the arguments *pro* and *con,* to observe how an idea first finds
lodgment in the brain, and to note the gradual sym-
metrical accretion of the fundamental nuclei for the
final creation — this is a privilege that has perhaps
[*sic*] never fully been realized by an observer.
" America is young and hopeful, at least; it is not
peopled, we are confidently assured, with soul-sick
tragedians mouthing their futile protests against the

113

Books in General

iron vice of environment, the ineradicable scar of heredity, the fell clutch of circumstance.

" Yet the reiterant ejaculations, the hyper-ethereal imaginings of the symbolist manner, are the symptoms of a tentative talent, not of an authoritative art."

I don't think Professor Henderson's remarks are ever quite meaningless, but I suspect that the most elephantine of them, if reduced to essentials, would be as commonplace as his more comprehensible statements that " Social criticism is the sign manual of the age," and that " the emancipation of woman, in the completest sense, is on the way "— which last gets a whole paragraph to itself. But it is pleasant to read it all; to see " Ibsen, Pinero, or Phillips " thus bracketed; to learn that Wilde's father was also " the father of modern otology," and to be told that Maeterlinck's " eternal prayer " is, " Oh, that this too, too solid flesh would melt "! That is on page 203; but the effect is somewhat marred by the fact that precisely the same " cry " has been, on page 37, attributed to Strindberg. Personally I plump for Maeterlinck.

"Another Century, and then . . ."

THERE is a certain sort of dull criticism which Dr. Johnson admirably stigmatized when he said that " there is no great merit in telling how many plays have ghosts in them and how this ghost is better than that." A great deal of American (not to speak of German) academic criticism belongs to this category; and especially those theses which are written by postgraduate students and candidates for the doctor's degree. These persons, when they are not exhuming dead reputations from well-deserved sepulchres, show an uncanny ingenuity in inventing original classifications and instituting unnecessary comparisons. But now and again such students manage to produce some enlightening piece of " research " work, and *The French Revolution and the English Novel* (Putnams) is one of the best of its kind. It is by Allene Gregory; and as I cannot tell from the name whether she is a gentleman or a lady, I shall call him Miss.

" This study in the *tendenz* novel was begun with the idea of paralleling Dr. Hancock's book, *The French Revolution and the English Poets.*" That

Books in General

is the first sentence of the preface, and it has a strictly academic flavour about it. The book is a " scientific " treatise; it would not have been written, so to say, either by a French Revolutionary or by an English novelist. If it dealt with the purely literary merits, which are few, of its subjects, it would be a useless sort of book. But its real purpose is to supply a chapter to the history of ideas, and especially Liberal political and social ideas. Many people talk as though they thought that the novel which canvasses the " problems " of sex, property, and religion were an invention of the last thirty years; and many others are under the impression that Charles Dickens was the first person to use fiction — though not, of course, the first person to employ fictions — for the promotion of legislation. Books about Godwin and Mary Wollstonecraft are occasionally written; and quite recently Thomas Holcroft, one of the chief of our Revolutionary novelists, was given considerable notice in Mr. Brailsford's excellent little book in the Home University Library. But, as far as my experience goes, there seem to be very few who know that England produced a century ago a whole group of novelists whose principal aim was not to " tell a straightforward story " or make the flesh creep, but to blow up the foundations of society with the gunpowder in the jam.

Miss Gregory's book is very comprehensive. Her principal figures are Holcroft, Godwin, and

Robert Bage; and she gives synopses of all their
novels, with extracts illustrating their doctrines.
Holcroft, one of the most lovable figures in the history of English democracy, was the sort of man who
is regarded as an obscure crank in his lifetime, then
forgotten for a time, and ultimately recognized as a
person of historical importance. He lived a long
life, and harmed nobody in the course of it. As a
stable-boy in a racing stable he read Addison, Bun-
yan, and Swift (whose tribute to the Houyhnhnms
must have had a local colour for him) ; he was afterwards a strolling actor, a hack writer, translator,
novelist, and playwright, one of his plays being
The Road to Ruin. When the Society for Consti-
tutional Reformation was raided Holcroft was arrested with Thomas Hardy and Horne Tooke, and
it was alleged against him, as justification for a
charge of high treason, that he had extolled moral
as against physical force. His associates being acquitted, he was never brought to trial: there comes
a point at which even a Government begins to feel
it is making an ass of itself. Holcroft's courage
never weakened " when Wordsworth, Coleridge,
Southey, and even Blake had recanted, and Godwin
and Paine had fallen silent, and all the world seemed
to have forgotten its vision of democracy." He
himself stated in terms: " Whenever I have under-
taken to write a novel I have proposed to myself a
specific moral purpose." His best novels are *Hugh
Trevor* and *Anna St. Ives.* In the latter the hero,

Books in General

Frank Henley, who shocks the orthodox by taking service rather than self-interest as his guiding principle, remarks:

" Let men look around and deny if they can that the present wretched system of each providing for himself instead of the whole for the whole does not inspire suspicion, fear, and hatred.   Well, well! — another century, and then . . ."

Just a century has passed.

Of Godwin's novels *Caleb Williams* is the only one that is at all read nowadays.   In spite of its impossibilities of character and action, it is a very good tract, especially where it deals with the prison system.   Miss Gregory's extracts from *Caleb Williams* might have been more profuse; but she gives interesting accounts of *St. Leon* and *Fleetwood*.   In the first of these a gentleman who possesses the philosopher's stone breaks into long reflections on " gold *versus* actual wealth "; in the other there are eloquent passages about the horrors of child-slavery in factories which anticipate the factory reports of a generation later, and which were so much in advance of their time that they still hold good in reference to certain of the States of America.   Godwin saw the whole thing very clearly: the pale, emaciated child given the free man's right of selling his labour at his own price in the open market and,

"Another Century, and then . . ."

as Godwin put it, able to earn salt to his bread at four, but unable to earn bread to his salt at forty. The placid Bage's novels were admired by Walter Scott. The most original is *Hermsprong, or Man as he is not,* the hero of which — who enters civilized society after being brought up among the Red Indians, and quails at the change — criticizes institutions with something of the tone of the versatile Mr. Smilash in *An Unsocial Socialist.*

Shelley's *Zastrozzi* and *St. Irvyne* are only interesting, if interesting at all, because they were written by their author. Miss Gregory ploughs through them, and also through the novels of Charlotte Smith, Mrs. Inchbald, and Mrs. Opie. She has a very interesting chapter on Mary Wollstonecraft and the early Women's Rights authors. I find most alluring the bare mention made of a certain Ann Plumptre, a novelist of whom I had never previously heard, who admired Napoleon enthusiastically. In 1810, according to Crabb Robinson,

" she declared she would welcome him if he invaded England because he would do away with aristocracy and give the country a better government."

Finally Miss Gregory has given space to the anti-revolutionary novelists, especially George Walker and Charles Lucas, of *The Infernal Quixote.* Ridicule of visionaries and demagogues through the me-

dium of novels was a recognized sport then as now;
and Lucas instituted an elaborate comparison between political and religious revivalists. A good
bibliography rounds off a very laudable compilation
which should interest all persons of subversive views
and direct the reading of the curious into some very
agreeable channels.

Herrick

MR. F. W. MOORMAN has edited for the Oxford Press a new edition of Herrick, which should supersede all its predecessors. There is very little editorial matter; Mr. Moorman has already written a *Life,* and his introduction and notes have a purely textual reference. The text, which is as satisfactory a one as we are likely to get, is based upon a collation of various divergent copies of the first edition; for Herrick appears to have hung about the printer's making alterations whilst the sheets were going through the press. And a full list is given of variants which occur in other printed copies of some of the poems and in MSS., of which the editor records several which have not previously been dealt with.

Any one who regards Herrick as an unsophisticated warbler pouring forth profuse strains of unpremeditated art may study these variants and correct himself. Mr. Moorman — I suppose he has sufficient reason, though he leaves one to guess what it is — assumes that the versions in MSS. and anthologies, etc., including those published after the *Hesperides,* are all earlier than the versions in the *Hesperides.* Now and then one is sorry that this should be so, as when the presumably earlier

Books in General

And night will come when men will swear
Time has spilt snow upon your haire,

is changed into

And time will come when you shall weare
Such frost and snow upon your haire.

But almost invariably the changes are improvements; and they are exceedingly numerous. Sometimes alterations in almost every line of a poem may be studied; sometimes there is a whole series of attempts at a line; and if we had more of Herrick's original MSS. available, we should no doubt find every poem a mass of trial trips and deletions. He blotted, filed, and pumice-stoned as much as any English poet, and he had the most delicate and deliberate sense of all the complex mechanism of verse. This rubicund Royalist rector was above all else a craftsman and a connoisseur.

What distinguishes his best — they are so well known that I need not quote them — poems from his second best is usually that the former have some especially taking touch of tenderness. It is never very deep; even in an epitaph he is more concerned with turning it well than with the, often apocryphal, death of the person commemorated. His adorations and griefs are as light as rose-leaves, but they are genuine in their way, and it is rather a slight difference in the quality of his emotion than a rela-

Herrick

tive superiority of craftsmanship that distinguishes his most perfect lyrics. His strongest characteristic, one that runs through the whole body of his verse, was his intense sensual appreciation of the material world. He was a connoisseur in life as in art. His admired record of the " liquefaction " of Julia's silks is characteristic of him. " O how that glittering taketh me! " he might have said of a thousand other things. He looked at colours and felt surfaces like a connoisseur; he tasted substances like an epicure tasting wines. He crushes all the distinctive hues and flavours out of flowers and spices, roses and primroses and violets, tulips, lilies, marigolds, cherryblossoms, virgins' skins, jet, ivory, amber, and gums. There is nothing romantic about him, and nothing dim; all things are equally vivid and clear, no thing is mysteriously vaster than other things. The moon and cream are both white — he will compare his lady's cheek to either indifferently or to both in a sentence; he relishes the loveliness of each and he drinks each, with exquisite pleasure, out of the same sized liqueur glass. Few other writers give one so keen a contact with the beauties of the physical world. But it is usually their sensuous appeal that is registered, sometimes their sentimental appeal, but never their mystic appeal. Herrick was a thoroughgoing pagan.

His capacity for conveying vivid impressions of the physical was not invariably employed upon such

Books in General

agreeable objects as daffodils and maidens. His sheer virtuosity made him compose those offensive epigrams which some bashful editors exclude from their collections. It is not to be supposed that he really wished to vent his spleen against Lungs, Gryll, Clasco, Scobble, Bunce, and his other, presumably pseudonymous, butts; though if his efforts in this direction got about in his Devonshire village and people took them to apply to themselves it is no wonder that the natives behaved towards him, as he complained, like surly savages. " Upon Batt " is one of the mildest of them:

> *Batt he gets children, not for love to reare 'em,*
> *But out of hope his wife might die to beare 'em.*

A more characteristic, but still a mild one, is " Upon Lungs ":

> *Lungs (as some say) ne'er sits him down to eate*
> *But that his breath do's Fly-blow all the meate.*

He tells — I refrain from the grossest ones — of another gentleman whose eyes were so sticky in the morning that his wife had to lick them open; of another whose raw eyes would supply an angler with a day's bait; and of another (very parsimonious) who preserved his nails, warts, and corns in boxes to make jelly for his broth. It is not astonishing that when the " sprightly Spartanesse " appeared to him in dream she remarked:

124

Herrick

Hence, Remove,
Herrick thou art too coorse for love.

But as one goes on through these things one is too
amused to be disgusted; one wonders what on earth
the man is going to think of next. And that was the
idea. He had compressed all the fragrance of the
spring into short lyrics — how much concentrated
beastliness could he get into a couplet? He had
rivalled Horace and Anacreon in one line; could he
rival Martial in another? You may picture him
making these things — sitting at a table in the sun
outside the rectory, quaffing, as was his wont, a social
tankard with his favourite pig, and working and
working at these singular concoctions until there
came the thrill of the artist who knows he has produced a perfect cameo.

His outlook and methods being such, it is not surprising that when he gave up his " unbaptized
Rhimes " and took to " Noble Numbers " he was
comparatively unsuccessful. Quaintness and neatness do not go far in religious verse, and the con-
genital materialism of Herrick's imagery sometimes
produced the most grotesque effects.

God is all forepart, for we never see
Any part backward in the Deitie.

An epigram which might have had some point if

125

Books in General

applied to a man is merely vapid when applied to the Deity.   And the vapid becomes comic in

> *I crawle, I creep; my Christ I come*
> *To thee, for curing Balsamum,*

and

> *Lord, I confesse, that thou alone are able*
> *To purifie this my Augean stable;*
> *Be the Seas water, and the Land all Sope,*
> *Yet if thy Bloud not wash me, there's no hope.*

Herrick was not an exalted religious poet.   But it doesn't much matter what he was not; what he was is one of the greatest small masters in the history of verse.

The Muse in Liquor

IN former times men wrote about drinking without the slightest self-consciousness. Our forefathers, from Teos to Chertsey, from Greenland's icy mountains to India's coral strand, sang the praises of what nobody in those days dreamt of calling alcohol, as they sang the praises of the other amenities of life. To Homer " bright wine " was as indispensable a commodity as bread: no home could be complete without it. If Anacreon and Horace were rather more sophisticated about it and tasted their liquor with a deliberate and spun-out sensuality, they still had no idea that there was anything morally questionable about drink. So onwards to mediæval times. When the Anglo-Saxon leech laid it down that if a man has fainted from hunger one should

" pull his locks from him, and wring his ears, and twitch his whiskers; when he is better give him some bread broken in wine,"

there was no rival school of leeches to jump up and protest that to inject alcoholic poisons into a debili-tated frame was about the worst thing you could do. Drinking in the Middle Ages was unchallengeably

127

respectable. " The introduction of wine and viticulture," says Mr. A. L. Simon in his history of the *Wine Trade in England,*

" is coeval with the introduction of the Christian religion. As the numbers of clergy increased, greater supplies of wine were required, so vines were planted at home, and a considerable foreign wine trade came into being."

The drinking-songs of the Middle Ages were largely composed by theological students, and it was (at least I am of that party which maintains that it was) an archdeacon of the English Church who wrote one of the two best lyrics of the kind that this island has produced — that perfect song in which he expresses the hope that he shall meet his latter end in a hostelry and that some one should hold a pottle-pot before his dying eyes:

> *Ut dicant cum venerint angelorum chori*
> *" Deus sit propitius huic potatori."*

Our other great song has also been attributed to an ecclesiastic, Bishop Still.

But if a modern bishop wrote a song about hot whisky, he would get into hot water. Times have changed. When a modern English king wants to do the popular thing, he takes the pledge; when

The Muse in Liquor

Henry III wanted to, he gave his old wine to the poor — the gift was not so noble as it sounds, for in his day old wine was bad, owing to the lack of glass bottles and well-made casks. Bishop Still, when he wrote (if he wrote) about the ale-swallowing capacity of himself and Tib, his wife, was on the safe side, for his sovereign lady, Queen Elizabeth, was addicted herself. Her Ministers had a job keeping her supplied with beer. When she was on one of her royal progresses, the Earl of Leicester wrote to Lord Burleigh:

" There is not one drop of good drink for her. We were fain to send to London and Kenilworth and divers other places where ale was; her own bere was so strong as there was no man able to drink it."

But since that time a question of principle has arisen, and the changed attitude of society towards drink has been accompanied by a corresponding change in the tone of those who write in praise of drink. They used to be natural and expository; they are now self-conscious and on the defensive.

I note the transition in a volume (1862) called *How to Mix Drinks, or The Bon-Vivant's Companion*, by Jerry Thomas, formerly principal bartender at the Metropolitan Hotel, New York, and the Planter's House, St. Louis. It is an ingenious book and a suitable companion to its shelf-neighbour, *The Maltworm's Vade-mecum,* a guide to the public-houses of early Georgian London. But if Mr. Thomas had been a contemporary of his brother connoisseur, it would never have occurred to him to write a preface apologizing for the mere compilation of such a book:

" Whether it is judicious that mankind should continue to indulge in such things, or whether it would be wiser to abstain from all enjoyments of that character, it is not our province to decide. We leave that question to the moral philosopher. We simply contend that a relish for ' social drinks ' is universal; that those drinks exist in greater variety in the United States than in any other country in the world, and that he, therefore, who proposes to impart to those drinks not only the most palatable but the most wholesome characteristics of which they may be made susceptible, is a genuine public benefactor."

You see the uneasiness coming in; the devotee is conscious of a disapproving eye. And what was perceptible in 1862 is much more marked to-day, when a considerable percentage of the population looks askance at a man who has been seen coming out of a bar, and when most of our priests and half our politicians denounce fermented drinks as an invention of the Devil. The results of this are seen in the twentieth-century Bacchanal's writings. He is

The Muse in Liquor

on the defensive. He cannot write a mere song in praise of drink: his Muse is largely, even mainly, concerned with dispraise of the opponents of drink. Mr. Belloc and Mr. Chesterton, belauding drinks as against beverages, strike an attitude which Anacreon simply would not have understood. They cannot lie and lap their liquor in dreamy content. Whenever they take up a pot of beer they have to march out and drink it defiantly in the middle of the Strand. It is almost as if they knew they were the champions of a lost, though noble, cause; and felt that at any moment they might be called upon to Die in the Last Tankard.

This tendency is strongly marked in Mr. Chesterton's volume *Wine, Water, and Song.* Mr. Chesterton spends half his time in abusing abstemious American and English millionaires, tea, cocoa, mineral waters, and grocers — who, lacking the genial proclivities of publicans, have never been known

> *To crack a bottle of fish sauce*
> *Or stand a man a cheese.*

But the novelty of tone makes the songs all the better: for the old material of drinking-songs was getting threadbare. To my thinking, these songs — most of them appeared in *The Flying Inn,* and it was a pity that they were omitted from the volume of collected *Poems* recently issued — are

131

amongst the finest bibulous songs ever written, and some of Mr. Chesterton's very best work. You can read them aloud to other people and very seldom come across a stilted or obscure phrase which makes you feel sheepish to say it. But, more than that, *Wine and Water, The Good Rich Man, The Song against Songs,* and the two poems on the English Road are the sort of infectiously musical things that one learns by heart without knowing one has done it.

Old Noah he had an ostrich farm and fowls on the largest scale,
He ate his eggs with a ladle in an egg-cup big as a pail,
And the soup he took was Elephant Soup, and the fish he took was whale,
But they all were small to the cellar he took when he set out to sail,
And Noah he often said to his wife when he sat down to dine,
" I don't care where the water goes if it doesn't get into the wine."

Lives there a man with soul so dead that when he comes across this or *The Road to Roundabout* (which is about the best of the lot) he does not automatically improvise a tune to it and start, according to his ability, singing it?

£5 Misspent

ANY one who is interested in what nobody has yet asked us to call the British language must have felt apprehensive if he read the correspondence recently printed in the *Times* on the subject of a synonym for the word " Colonial." It appears that this word is " strongly objected to " in the — er — Dominions, and especially in Canada. The Central Committee of the Overseas Club therefore started a Missing Word Competition. It offered a prize of £5 for the best synonym and " members have been most prolific in their ideas." The examples given of their fecundity are, however, so malformed as to lead to the hope that in future they will practise an intellectual Malthusianism. The Chairman of the Club says that amongst the terms suggested are Britainer, Britonial, Imperialist, Dominion, Britannian, Britoner, Greater Briton, Anglian Pan-Briton, and such repulsive composts as Empirean, Transmarine (why not Ultramarine?), Away-Born, Out-Briton, Co-Briton, Albionian, Mac-Briton, and Britson. What those which he does not publish were like one can only surmise; but no doubt Ap-Briton, O'Briton, Britidian, Britkinson, Dominisher, Fraternanglian, Nonsunsetton, and Heptathalassian were among them. And so, possibly, was Oversear.

Books in General

It needs must be that new words should come; and one should not cry woe against those through whom they come. We are constantly inventing or importing words to convey ideas or shades of feeling for which we previously had no exact means of expression. We also necessarily acquire new words for new objects, such as chemicals and machines. When men made the telephone they had to call it something; and the same thing applied to the omnibus. We can frequently trace new words to their inventors. But we may safely say that successful new words are seldom " made up " cold-bloodedly merely for the sake of the thing. An author hits upon a word half-accidentally, developing it usually from some word already familiar; or a philosopher or scientist constructs one out of fragments of Greek, or Latin, or Greek and Latin mixed, because he has a new object to describe. The process is going on continually. The rivals " airman " and " aviator " (somebody once asked if you could call a miner a " talpiator ") are at present* fighting it out in the Press and on men's tongues; and if some central authority is in the future established over the heads of the sovereign Powers, it is likely that the word " supernational," now being bruited about, may come into use to describe it. We may get in time, too, an inclusive word which will imply " citizen of the British Empire," covering both Britons (or, if you prefer it, Britirish) and Colonials. But I doubt

*Airman happily seems (July 1918) to have won.— S. E.

134

£5 Misspent

whether such a word will result from a public competition.

When it comes it will come because some one person starts using it and others take to it. And when it is a case of inventing a synonym, a new word as a substitute for an old one in general use, I think it most unlikely that a group of persons such as the Overseas Club could persuade the race to abandon a universally used word like "Colonial" for some £5 prize word merely because hypersensitive people think that the word used to have a faintly derogatory flavour. "Colonial" is very strongly entrenched. One can just understand how the Americans have come to use the abominable word "Britisher" instead of the ancient "Briton"; for it falls more trippingly off the tongue. But "Colonial" is a most liquid, easy, and euphonious word. If it is ever superseded, it will be so because some other word comes in with the larger connotation to which I have referred, a word which is bound to come into being when we cease to think of the Empire as composed of the United Kingdom on the one hand and the Colonies on the other, but think of it as a federation of equal and distinct units.

It is a pity that people take so seriously the fact that when the words "Colonies" and "Colonial" were first used by us they had certain associations. For it is evident that to the vast majority of our countrymen they are entirely divested of them. Whatever one's habits, one automatically thinks when the word " Colonial " is mentioned, not of a humble emigrant who wants shepherding, but of a person who is the very quintessence of independence. Any one who has even the most superficial acquaintance with the language knows that words can lose their old associations utterly. If, for example, I were arrested and charged for alleging, in a public speech, one of our Royal Princes to be " a silly knave," I should not find the magistrate very sympathetic if I said I was using the words in a Shakespearean (which in this case would be equivalent to a Pickwickian) sense, and that I merely meant to call him " a simple boy." Similarly, where an object changes its form its name changes its connotation. If one could talk of a bottle to a mediæval ancestor, he would think of something made of leather; to-day a bottle is essentially something made of glass. If we always wanted a new term directly a new association was created, there would be no end to the process; we should have to have a Ministry of Constructive Philology always at work. After all, Charleston was named after an English king when the North American plantations were very subordinate indeed; and Melbourne after a member of the British House of Lords, an institution of which few modern Australians approve. So, on the whole, saving the Overseas Club's reverence, we may as well, for the time being, stick to " Colonial."

136

Shakespeare's Women and Mr. George Moore

HANDLING the Porcupine of Avon is always ticklish work. When Mr. George Moore, after containing himself for years, at last wrote to explain that it was he, and not Mr. Shaw or Mr. Franz Heinrichs, who discovered the fact that Shakespeare's female characters were weak because they were written for boy-actors, it was only natural that another correspondent should show that Mr. Moore had been forestalled by an eighteenth-century Frenchman. Mr. Moore's remark about the boy-actors was, however, merely a passing observation in a lecture in French (published in the *Revue Bleue* in 1910) which is an important document in the movement against what Mr. Shaw calls Bardolatry.

" He is inconceivably wise; the others conceivably." Thus Emerson; and a few generations of such sweeping remarks were bound to be followed by a reaction. For a hundred years we have swallowed Shakespeare steadily and swallowed him whole; a man has even written a book on *The Messiahship of Shakespeare*. And of all his powers,

137

that of creating an infinite variety of female character has been perhaps more enthusiastically praised
than any other. The professors have given us
treatises on Shakespeare's Feminine Types; and the
less erudite public has been deluged with Posies
from Shakespeare's Garden of Girls. " O Nature!
O Shakespeare! which of ye drew from the other? "
That is typical. Dr. Lewes, one of the ablest German writers on the subject, kneels and adores, and
asks women to do the same. " This piece," he says
of *Henry VIII,*

" this piece and its female characters should indeed
inspire women with profound gratitude towards a
poet who represents a queen and a heroine who is
above all things an excellent woman, displaying in
the midst of frightful trials all the best womanly
qualities, thus proving that a noble, pure feminine
heart is the home of the noblest virtue, the highest
truth and purity. Seldom has more flattering homage been paid to the sex than by Shakespeare in his
presentation of Catherine of Aragon."

And hear Mrs. Jamieson, author of the best-known
English book on these women. Dare any one apply
the epithet " clever " to Portia, " this heavenly com-
pound of talent, feeling, wisdom, beauty, and gentle-
ness "? As for Lady Macbeth, with her " Gothic
grandeur, rich chiaroscuro, and deep-toned colours,"
even she is not to be insulted by comparison with

138

other villainesses. Sophocles' Clytemnestra had been mentioned, but

"would any one compare this shameless adulteress, cruel murderess and unnatural mother with Lady Macbeth? *Lady Macbeth herself would certainly shrink from the approximation.*"

One *has* sometimes felt that her ladyship was probably president of the local branches of the G.F.S. and the Soldiers' and Sailors' Families Association.

There was nothing of this sort about Mr. George Moore's lecture. It opened with a strong protest against the "vast clamour" of Shakespeare's worshippers:

"One might take them for a gathering of negro Methodists in a chapel, each one straining his lungs to out-bellow his neighbour, in order to attract the Almighty's attention. Is it that the critics think that Shakespeare is listening to them? At any rate, the madness increases daily, and, if the cult of Jahveh should happen to decay in England, I should not be surprised were they to promote Shakespeare to the vacant throne in the heavens."

After this engaging beginning he went on to the general contention that neither Shakespeare nor any of his contemporaries drew or painted a real woman. The Renaissance was interested in women only as

139

queens or odalisques, and Shakespeare at most made a few delicious silhouettes of women. His men were another matter. " Hamlet is the secret thought of all men "; and, though it hurts Mr. Moore to agree with Tolstoi, he reaffirmed Tolstoi's statement that " Falstaff is the most universal and original thing in Shakespeare." " Hamlet is the hieroglyphic and symbol of the intellect; Falstaff is the symbol and arabesque of the flesh." But Shakespeare, like Balzac, was chiefly concerned with " the eternal masculine."

But suppose it be admitted that Shakespeare has no female Hamlet and no female Falstaff; is it not arguable that then the case for the superiority of Shakespeare's males over his females is very much less strong? It would be absurd to attempt to dogmatize on the subject; but personally I doubt whether any one who cannot get inside the minds of most (though many would exempt Heine's " ancient Parisienne " Cleopatra, and one or two more) of Shakespeare's women will get inside the minds of most of his men either. When Professor Dowden said that he had " edited a whole play for love of Imogen " the remark (if he heard it) may have sounded strange to Mr. Moore; but would he understand, either, any one editing a whole play for love of Antonio, Bassanio, Benedict, the Duke of *Twelfth Night,* King Lear, Othello, Mark Antony, or Henry V? It is possible to hold the view that

140

Shakespeare's Women and Mr. G. Moore

Shakespeare " put himself " into a few characters and observed the others " from the outside," making them most interesting when they are most markedly what are called " character parts." Personally, though I should certainly know Hamlet or Falstaff if I met them in swallowtails, I don't think there are many other of Shakespeare's characters whom I should recognize if I encountered them clothed in other than their traditional garments. But I do not think it is easy to sustain the argument that, as a whole, his women are less carefully and sympathetically drawn than his men — Lady Macbeth than Macbeth, Juliet than Romeo, Cleopatra than Anthony, Beatrice than Benedict, Rosalind than Orlando — or, still more, that he was not interested in women and regarded them in a casual lazy way as decorations. Shakespeare's politics were Heaven knows what; and he may not necessarily have drawn Portia as an argument for the admission of women to the Inns of Court. But one would have imagined that if ever there were a writer who treated women and men on a footing of complete equality, and even perhaps elevated women's moral superiority to an indefensible pitch, it was he. If his female characters are not living human beings it is certainly not because he despised them. He gave them plenty of virtue, wit, courage, and will, and an ample share of the stage; it is, with all due respect to Mr. Moore, grotesque to suggest that he thought of them merely as properties.

Books in General

The recent correspondence sent me back to Mr. Moore's paper, and I read it with admiration for the fruits of what he called a month's rather exhausting liaison with the French language. But something about it — perhaps it was the catalogue of heroines, each with an appropriate criticism — seemed familiar. I have tracked it; here also Mr. Moore has been anticipated. It was the late Max O'Rell — it is almost like being anticipated by Charley's Aunt — who remarked that

" The heroines of Shakespeare are for the most part slaves or fools. Juliet is a spoilt child, Desdemona a sort of submissive odalisque, Beatrice a chatterbox, and Ophelia a goose."

It is very difficult indeed to say anything new about Shakespeare.

Moving a Library

I DO not remember that any of our meditative
essayists has written on the subject of Moving
One's Books.   If such an essay exists I should
be glad to go to it for sympathy and consolation.
For I have just moved from one room to another, in
which I devoutly hope that I shall end my days,
though (as Mr. Asquith would put it in his rounded
way) " at a later, rather than at an earlier, date."
Night after night I have spent carting down two
flights of stairs more books than I ever thought I
possessed.   Journey after journey, as monotonously
regular as the progresses of a train round the Inner
Circle: upstairs empty-handed, and downstairs creep-
ing with a decrepit crouch, a tall, crazy, dangerously
bulging column of books wedged between my two
hands and the indomitable point of my chin.   The
job simply has to be done; once it is started there is
no escape from it; but at times during the process
one hates books as the slaves who built the Pyramids
must have hated public monuments.   A strong and
bitter book-sickness floods one's soul.   How ignominious to be strapped to this ponderous mass of
paper, print, and dead men's sentiments!   Would
it not be better, finer, braver, to leave the rubbish
where it lies and walk out into the world a free, un-
trammelled,   illiterate   Superman?   Civilization!

Books in General

Pah! But that mood is, I am happy to say, with me ephemeral. It is generated by the necessity for tedious physical exertion and dies with the need. Nevertheless the actual transport is about the briefest and least harassing of the operations called for. Dusting (or " buffeting the books," as Dr. Johnson called it) is a matter of choice. One can easily say to oneself, " These books were banged six months ago " (knowing full well that it was really twelve months ago), and thus decide to postpone the ceremony until everything else has been settled. But the complications of getting one's library straight are still appalling.

Of course, if your shelves are moved bodily it is all right. You can take the books out, lay them on the floor in due order, and restore them to their old places. But otherwise, if you have any sense of congruity and proportion, you are in for a bad time. My own case could not be worse than it is. The room from which I have been expelled was low and square; the room into which I have been driven is high and L-shaped. None of my old wall-shelves will fit my new walls; and I have had to erect new ones, more numerous than the old and totally different in shape and arrangement. It is quite impossible to preserve the old plan; but the devisal of another one brings sweat to the brow. If one happened to be a person who never desired to refer to his books the obvious thing to do would be to

144

Moving a Library

put the large books into the large shelves and the small ones into the small shelves and then go and smoke a self-satisfied pipe against the nearest post. But to a man who prefers to know where every book is, and who possesses, moreover, a sense of System and wishes everything to be in surroundings proper to its own qualities, this is not possible. Even an unsystematic man must choose to add a classification by subject to the compulsory classification by size; and, in my case, there is an added difficulty produced by a strong hankering for some sort of chronological order. There is nothing like that for easy reference. If you know that Beowulf will be at the left-hand end of the shelf that he fits and Julia Ward, the Sweet Singer of Michigan, at the right-hand end, you save yourself a good deal of time. But when your new compartments do not fit your old sections, when the large books of Stodge are so numerous as to insist upon intruding into the shelves reserved for large books of Pure Literature, and the duodecimos of Foreign Verse surge in a tidal wave over the preserves of the small books on Free Trade, Ethics, and Palæontology, one is reduced to the verge of despair. That is where I am at this moment; sitting in the midst of a large floor covered with sawdust, white distemper, nails, tobacco-ash, burnt matches, and the Greatest Works of the World's Greatest Masters. Fortunately, in Ruskin's words, " I don't suppose I shall do it again for months and months and months."

Table-Talk and Jest Books

SAMUEL BUTLER'S *Note-Books* have now gone into another (popular) edition, issued by Mr. Fifield. I don't know how large these editions are: if, as I fear, they run to less than fifty thousand copies apiece, Samuel Butler has not yet got his due. There is no other volume in the whole of his collected works to equal this selection from his note-books: you have here the quintessence of his wisdom, his taste, and his superb impudence. The book really belongs to the " table-talk " or " ana " class of books. Butler, that is to say, recorded his own table-talk. His principle was, he said, that if you wanted to record a thought you had to shoot it on the wing. If, therefore, he thought of or said anything especially illuminating or amusing, or heard any one else say anything of the sort, down it went. And it always went down as colloquially and freshly as if a Boswell had been present recording conversation with a faithful pen. Butler Boswellized himself. For Boswell's *Life,* as has been remarked before, is the greatest collection of " ana " in the language. It consisted of Johnson's table-talk strung on a biographical thread.

Personally I find it hard to draw the line be-

146

Table-Talk and Jest Books

tween general table-talk and anecdotes told of certain persons: most collections include both. But such works, of whatever kind, consisting of detached scraps of great men's wit, are an agreeable form of reading, and an old-established one. The Greeks possessed volumes of excerpts from people's conversation, and some Latin wrote a book, now unfortunately lost, under the piquant title of *De Jocis Ciceronis*. The great age of such collections began, however, with the Renaissance, when Poggio the Florentine collected his " facetiæ." My own extracts from Poggio are included in a German collection of 1603, all written in Latin, which gives also the " facetiæ " of other wits, notably of Nicodemus Frischlin of Balingen. This man was a German scholar of exceptional brilliance who finally, on being incarcerated for the last of many escapades, broke his neck trying to escape. We have no such University professors of classics now. " Ana " so-called begin with the *Scaligerana,* which gave the drastic conversation of the younger Scaliger as recorded by two of his disciples. The success of this led to a rush in France. Every one who had known an eminent man deceased rushed out with a volume of table-talk; *Thuana, Perroniana,* etc. The *Sorberiana* " sive excerpta ex ore Samuelis Sorbiere " was famous in its day, but I find it very dull. Much the best collection is *Menagiana,* " Bon Mots, Rencontres Agreables, Pensées Judicieuses, et Observations Curieuses de M. Ménage," of which the second edition (my copy) is dated 1694-5. This man was a scholar, knew everybody and had a sharp tongue: he is extremely good reading, though, nowadays, very little read. The contents of both of these books are arranged (as is Butler's) under subject-headings, in alphabetical order. The same order is observed in Selden's *Table-Talk*, the next best book of the kind to Boswell in our tongue. It was published after Selden's death by his private secretary, and is full of extraordinarily sensible and witty things. And, unlike many wits, Selden always possessed a sense of responsibility. He remarked himself (under heading "Wit," as he did not realize) that

" He that lets fly all he knows and thinks may by chance be satyrically witty. Honesty sometimes keeps a man from growing rich, and civility from being witty."

Few of the wits whose sayings are collected are so scrupulous. Our other classical example in the kind is Coleridge's *Table-Talk*, which is full of fine criticism, funny stories, and good epigrams.

These collections shade off into the ordinary jest book. After all, there is no clear division between stories told by a dead man and stories collected and published by a living one, between stories about one man and stories about fifty different men. When

Table-Talk and Jest Books

the new learning was still new, men had a mania for collecting pointed anecdotes about the eminent. The fattest book of the kind I know is Casper Ens's *Epidorpidum,* published at Cologne in the early seventeenth century. It is full of the remarks of Alexander to Diogenes and Pope Innocent to St. Vitus and the repartees of King Pyrrhus of Epirus to a recalcitrant phalanx. Right on into the eighteenth century works with titles like *Elite de Bon-Mots,* and full of such historical personages, were popular on the Continent. English jest books were perhaps more local and contemporary in their references. Our eighteenth-century ancestors were addicted to anecdotes about Mr. Quin and Mr. Foote and what the Duke of Wharton said to the Bishop. In our own time the larger, if not the smaller, public still shows some demand for collections of anecdotes of this sort: and popular weeklies of the *Answers* and *Tit-Bits* type usually seem to find it desirable to print columns of stories about Henry Irving, Mr. Gladstone, and such people. But it is a long way from *Tit-Bits* to Samuel Butler: which shows where one may land oneself if one does not know where to draw a firm line when shading-off is apparently gradual. I cannot review Butler at this time of day; but there are very few books existing which contain more sense to the square inch than this. Though the worst of his books is good reading, the *Note-Books* is as certainly his finest book as Boswell's *Johnson* is the finest of Johnson's.

Stephen Phillips

THE announcements of Stephen Phillips's death must have carried many people's thoughts backward. Me personally it took back to a time, years ago, when I was in the first flush of my youthful beauty and sitting out at a country dance. Coloured lamps burned between boughs, trees gently swished under a summer sky, the sound of violins and the glide of many feet penetrated softly from a distance; and a partner, whose face was shadowy pale in the faint light, sat clasping her knees, looking out into the night, and talking in a deep ecstatic voice of *Marpessa, Herod,* and *Paolo and Francesca.* It was not merely that she thought that I was that sort of person: the same thing was happening in every county in England. Phillips had the biggest boom that any English poet has had for a generation. The extravagance of the eulogies seems very strange now. There was scarcely a critic who did not lose his balance. I have just been looking up some of these panegyrics, and the pitch of them makes one feel a little sadly for a man who outlived so great and so early a fame. The history of literature was ransacked for comparisons. Chapman, Webster, Wordsworth, Shakespeare himself were brought in: and almost the most modest of

Stephen Phillips

the assessors was Mr. William Archer, who described Phillips as " the elder Dumas speaking with the voice of Milton." I remember the *Daily Mail* devoting its magazine page to a description of the poet, in the course of which it explained, with characteristic love of figures, that here was a man who had discovered how to make £1000 a year out of poetry. But it did not last. The climax of Phillips's success came with *Paolo and Francesca;* the subsequent plays were received with a diminuendo of warmth; and in the last few years he was comparatively ignored.

The early adoration was absurd but not incomprehensible. It was due, one might say, to the fact that Phillips was not an original writer. Much used to be made of a certain trick he had of accenting occasional lines of blank verse in a strange manner: on the strength of this he was treated as a revolutionary innovator in English prosody. In reality, in spite of this one peculiarity, he was anything but an innovator. He had an ear for the magniloquent progress of Milton's verse and the crooning music of Tennyson's; he had a great facility for reproducing them; and to those who are susceptible only to artistic effects which (though they are unconscious of it) remind them of effects previously experienced, he seemed, therefore, to be a consummate artist. He gave them precisely what they had learnt to desire and expect from a poet, the familiar splendours

151

Books in General

and the familiar silences, the familiar agonies and
the familiar tendernesses, the scents, the flowers, the
gems, the old words with their unmistakable associations, the brilliant single lines, with here and there
an alliteration and here and there an onomatopœia.
His work was not, of course, a *mere* compost. He
added something. His emotions, though not deep,
were genuine enough; he had a pretty fancy; and
he had a considerable knowledge of how to produce
effects on the stage. *Paolo and Francesca* was certainly in every way superior to most of the other
attempts which have been made in our time at stage-
plays in blank verse. It was effective in the theatre.
One remembers the excitement about the skilful ending: the murder behind the scenes, the bodies
brought in, the murderer's revulsion:

I did not know the dead could have such hair.
Hide them. They look like children fast asleep.

But those who did not shrink from comparing it
with *Romeo and Juliet* omitted to notice the same
deficiencies as appeared in all his work. He was
largely derivative and there was very little hard
brainwork behind his verse.

Herod, Ulysses, and *Nero* were all less well
made: the last two were panoramas. In all three
the author depended on succulent or flamboyant
" purple patches " for his effects, descriptions too

Stephen Phillips

full of redundant metaphor and violent outbursts of picturesque but too flimsy rhetoric.   There was little characterization in them, the persons were puppets in the hands of the contriver of stage spectacles: they were carried off by brilliant and exotic scenery and costumes, by the romantic language, and by the real and skilful, if conventional, melody of the verse. All the best qualities of Stephen Phillips, the qualities that gave people a thrill they were unaccustomed to in the theatre of his time, are quintessentialized in Herod's megalomaniac speeches and in the oratorical Marlowesque remark that one of the suitors in *Ulysses* made to Penelope:

Thou hast caught splendour from the sailless sea
And mystery from the many stars outwatched.

His defects were observed by few when he was a popular dramatist: but those readers who only know him by his later work will misjudge him if they think that he never had more power than he showed in that.   His more recent volumes, written in ill-health, would never have got him a reputation. Here and there the old bravura appeared, and there is a short lyric in the volume of 1913 which is certainly equal to anything in the early book of poems with which he made his name — and in which he showed signs of contact with the " movement " of the 'nineties.   But from most of these later poems the life had gone, leaving the imitative structure

153

naked to the eye. His last volume, *Panama and other Poems,* was issued just before he died by his original publisher, Mr. John Lane; and the way in which he had succumbed to his influences was very evident. Lines on the Canal such as

Chagres by Dam stupendous of Gatun

not merely remind one of Milton but are exact mechanical reproductions of Milton.

Incidentally the difficulties of literary biography are illustrated by his obituary notices. *My Daily News* gave his age as forty-nine, my *Times* gave it as fifty-one; and looking into the *Encyclopædia Britannica* to see which of these estimates it would confirm, I found that it alleged him to be forty-seven. *The Encyclopædia* says that he was at Queens' College, Cambridge, when he joined Mr. Benson's company; the *Times* that he was cramming at Scoones'. When we have this conflict of evidence about a contemporary who was known personally to hundreds of people in London, where are we with Elizabethans and Romans? Personally I believe that, in the matter of birth-dates, nothing is really reliable — not even a man's own statement — except public registers.

Gray and Horace Walpole

IF a gentleman in Calabria digs up with a spade a hitherto unknown fragment of the obscure Latin historian P. Pomponius Fatto there is great excitement about it, and research congratulates itself upon its achievements. I can quite appreciate the feeling. All treasure-trove is exciting. The smallest recovery from the long-buried past is worth having; it may, in itself, fill a gap somewhere and encourages the hope of greater finds. But why not make just as much of a palaver about Dr. Paget Toynbee's disinterment of nearly a hundred " new " letters by the poet Gray? The new letters are included in *The Correspondence of Gray, Walpole, West, and Ashton* (Oxford University Press, 2 vols.); and they were found in the collection of Captain Sir F. E. Waller, who was recently killed in action, and to whose memory the volume is dedicated. Gray, Horace Walpole, Richard West, and Thomas Ashton formed a " Quadruple Alliance " at Eton. West went on to Oxford, the other three to Cambridge. We get first of all an exchange between all four; then West dies, in his twenties; then, years afterwards, relations with Ashton are broken; and, finally, there is a long series that passed between Walpole and Gray up to the time of

the poet's death in 1771.   In all there are 248 letters; of these 153 were written by Gray, eighty-nine
of which have never been published before.   Others
have never before been printed in full, and few
have escaped maltreatment by previous editors.
Their errors ranged from deliberate alteration,
truncation, and blending to bad transcription and un-
intelligent acceptance.   How easily the most comic
errors may creep into a text where each editor ne-
glects to use, or has not access to, original sources
may be shown by the history of a single word.
Gray wrote a Latin poem about the god of Love in
which one line began " Ludentem fuge."   This
was printed by Miss Berry as " Sudentem fuge ";
and this has been " corrected " by subsequent editors
into *" Sudantem fuge "!*

The characters of the correspondents come out
very clearly.   Even when, just after they have left
school, they are all writing rather affectedly (and
with a plethora of classical quotation), Ashton is
obviously the one fundamentally insincere member
of the group.   He is hyperself-conscious, nastily artificial.   Later on he even refers in Joseph Surface's
very own words to his " noble sentiments ": this was
clearly the man to make, by his double-dealing, the
temporary breach between Gray and Walpole, and,
ultimately, to compel Walpole to cast him off by his
incivility when Walpole was no longer useful to him.
Richard West, son of an Irish Lord Chancellor, has

Gray and Horace Walpole

no apparent defect save excessive seriousness. There is a touch of the priggish mixed with the high-mindedness and generosity of this able young invalid; but one can understand Gray's devotion to him. Some of the poetry of his here given (he appeared in Dodsley's *Miscellany* by the way) is surprisingly good. He was the Arthur Hallam of the eighteenth century.

The Walpole letters are, as always, unsurpassable of their kind. His undergraduate letter (in parody of Addison's descriptions of Italy) relating a journey from London to Cambridge, is admirable; but the letters describing his continental tour with Gray are better, and those, still later, about the *beau monde* of Paris are perfect. There is a peculiar charm too about the correspondence with Gray as to the details and publication of his works, the half-solemn, half whimsical concentration on the tiny antiquarian details to which each was addicted, the eager little controversies and explorations, the odd little jokes. But though Gray, taking his correspondence as a whole, considering both volume, range, and formal excellence, cannot contest Walpole's position as the greatest of English letter-writers, there is a flavour about his letters that makes them peculiarly delightful. Walpole writes fully dressed, though with exquisite manner; Gray writes naturally, and without obvious reserve sometimes even gambolling. There

157

Books in General

may be people, familiar with Gray only through
his elevated and sombre verse, who fancy him
an exceedingly self-contained and formal man,
who feel (like the person who greatly amused him
by addressing him as " The Rev. T. Gray ") that
he simply *must* have been a divine. There were certainly contemporaries of his who met him and got
the impression that he was constitutionally grave,
reticent, aloof. His letters show that he was anything but that to his friends. The author of the
Elegy habitually " played the goat." There are a
whole string of skit letters here: in one he writes
to Walpole as " Honner'd Nurse," addressing the
illiterate screed " to mie Nuss att London "; in another he wallows in Oriental imagery about the
dew of the morning; in another he applies to stag-
nant Cambridge a whole long passage from Isaiah
describing deserted Babylon, the home of dragons
and haunt of screech-owls. He had a great habit
of ending his letters with something openly idiotic.
Once he bursts out with " Pray, did you ever see an
elephant? "; another time his peroration is:

" The Assizes are just over. I was there; but
I a'nt to be transported. Adieu! "

and another excursion concludes with a ludicrous
burlesque of the type of commonplaces usually to be
found in letters:

" There is a curious woman here that spins Glass,

158

and makes short Aprons and furbelow'd petticoats
of it, a very genteel wear for summer, & discover's
all the motions of the limbs to great advantage.
She is a successour of Jack, the Aple dumpling Spin-
ner's: my Duck has eat a Snail &c.: & I am — yours
sincerely   T. G."

Those who think of poets as persons without humour
who live in a permanent exaltation and are quite
unlike reasonable beings will be shocked with Gray's
remarks when he had, to the publisher's alarm, with-
drawn a poem from his forthcoming small volume:

" but to supply the place of it in bulk, lest my work
should be mistaken for the works of a flea or a
pismire, I promised to send him an equal weight of
poetry or prose: so, since my return hither, I put
up about two ounces of stuff: viz.   The Fatal Sis-
ters, The Descent of Odin . . . with all this I shall
be but a shrimp of an author."

On a night nine years before this, General Wolfe,
as his boat crept towards the Quebec bank of St.
Lawrence, had recited the *Elegy* to his companions
and told them that he had rather have written that
poem than take Quebec.

Gray's judgments on other authors (though he
was unjust to the more fermentative kind of Frenchman) were uniformly good.   He suspected Ossian,
but hoped he was a fraud for the sake of the jest.

Books in General

If, he said, Macpherson had done it all to hoax fools, " I would undertake a journey into the Highlands only for the pleasure of seeing him." He read Boswell's early book on Corsica and almost prophetically observed:

" The pamphlet proves what I have always maintained, that any fool may write a most valuable book by chance, if he will only tell us what he heard and saw with veracity."

In politics he was interested only mildly, but he liked to gossip about them. " Do oblige me," he writes to Walpole,

" with a change in the Ministry: I mean, something one may tell, that looks as if it were near at hand; or if there is no truth to be had, then a good likely falsehood for the same purpose. I am sorry to be so reduced."

" A good likely falsehood ": is it not in perpetual demand?

A Horrible Bookseller

PEOPLE often complain that booksellers know too little about the goods they sell. If only, the argument is, books were sold by men of taste, familiar with their contents, the public would buy more good literature: as things are, the blind bookseller leads the blind customer. There is something in this. An educated bookseller can actually educate other people. Many intelligent young persons reach the age of twenty-one without having met a single person with the habit of good reading, and do not " get on to " literature because it has never been suggested to them that they will like it. Booksellers may act as teachers. There are booksellers, though not many, who make a practice of " nursing " promising young customers, gradually cultivating their taste until they become confirmed book-lovers and book-buyers. One such complained to me not long ago that he had had scores of likely colts taken away from him by Lord Kitchener, and did not know how many of them would come back. That is an ideal sort of man for the trade in modern literature. One might say, in fact, that in a perfect world (from the book-buyer's point of view) the dealers in new books would know everything about books, and the dealers in old books would know

Books in General

nothing whatever about them. The point of this
last subsection is obvious, but the other day I had an
experience that greatly fortified my view. I had
often met the second-hand bookseller whose learning prevented one from buying anything cheap from
him; I have now encountered one whose interest
in his subject prevented one from buying anything
at all.

He was not so much a really learned man as a
man with what is called " an inexhaustible fund of
information." It is quite possible that if he had
had a real rarity in his shop he would have known
nothing about it. But about the promiscuity of his
reading there was no doubt. When I entered the
shop he was seated at a table absorbing something
that looked as if it might be the Travels of Living-
stone or Speke. His spectacles were on his fore-
head, his elbows on the table, his hands in his hair;
and his beard almost touched his book. " Do you
mind if I go through? " I said. " Sairtainly," he
said, betraying his origin. " And what may you be
interested in? " " Oh . . . books," I replied
vaguely. " That is a verra conseederable category," he observed. Was it poetry I liked? he went
on. I murmured " Yes," and he led me to the
place where he kept it. But before I had got my
fingers on a book he made it evident that it was
he and not I that was going to have the " look

round." Here, for example, was a volume of Kirke
White. Had I ever read him? How wonderful
was that hymn (quoted at length) of his! What a
career! He was a butcher's son and a lawyer's
clerk. He had a gift for mathematics, and they
gave him a sizarship at Cambridge. He would
have been one of the greatest figures in English
literature had he lived. Was I interested in Italian
books? Well, then, perhaps I would like a good
copy of (!!!) *I Promessi Sposi*. It was extraordinary the number of copies of that book which must
have been printed. But there was no supply without
a demand.

I tried in vain to check the torrent with some
sort of remark which, though polite, might, nevertheless, have an air of finality. It was no good.
My fingers never got beyond touching the back of
a book before he had taken down another, pulled
me round, and fixed me with a glittering eye for
which the Ancient Mariner himself would have been
tempted to offer a large sum. Godwin, now. Did
I like *Caleb Williams?* Yes, of course! But had
I read his History of England? It was by way of
being a reply to Clarendon. Clarendon was a great
writer. But he was not impartial. And the worst
of it was that he seemed to be impartial when he was
most unfair. When he was sacrificing everything
for his King he little thought how his loyalty would

163

be rewarded. He was too moral for Charles II; but, what was worse, he kept the purse-strings too tight. He would not give him money for one of his mistresses. Was it Barbara Palmer? No, it was not Barbara Palmer, and it was not Nelly Gwyn. At any rate, it was one of them. And when, in the end, the grant was made to her, she died before she got the money!

This appeared to amuse the old man. When he had laughed himself out, it was to resume with some work, dated 1784, which contained a recipe for making a Prime Minister: the chief ingredients being hypocrisy, mendacity, corruption, and cant. This opened up a large field of speculation. Who was Premier in 1784? Why, of course, it was young Billy Pitt! ("Yes," I said.) No, it was Rockingham. ("Yes," I said.) No, it wasn't; it was Bute. So it proceeded. I spent, in all, two hours in that shop; in the course of which time I had stolen glances at about six worthless books. For all I know it was as full of gems of purest ray serene as are the dark unfathomed caves of ocean. I left without making a single purchase, and the proprietor seemed quite hurt at this unfriendly response to his attentions. How that old man earns his living I don't know. I think he must have private means. But in future I shall have a warmer feeling than ever for the sort of red-nosed second-hand bookseller, now, unfortunately, not very com-

A Horrible Bookseller

mon, who knows only the outsides of books, and
who sits smoking on a heap of rubbish in the corner
of his shop with the air of a tramp resting on a
roadside pile of stones.

The Troubles of a Catholic

BEING at the moment in bed with influenza, I was at once incapable of intellectual effort and in need of spiritual sustenance. I had therefore been reading a little Theology. The more modern works of the kind in my possession are at once too profound in thought and too arid in phraseology, so I worked rapidly backwards. One never knows what one is going to come across, and in the beginning of *A Just Discharge to Dr. Stilling-fleet's Unjust Charge of Idolatry Against the Church of Rome with a Discovery of the Vanity of his late Defense in his Pretended Answer to a Book Entitled Catholicks No Idolaters By way of Dialogue Between Eunomius, a Conformist, and Catharinus, a Nonconformist*, I struck a very pathetic thing. The work was written, I believe, by the Catholic controversialist Godden, and published in 1677. At that time it was difficult for Catholics to get anything out in England, and this work was published at Paris. Hence the unhappy author's statement about " Errata ":

" The English Press being watch'd of late, as the Orchard of the Hesperides was of old, and a necessity arising from thence of making use of a Paris

The Troubles of a Catholic

Printer, who understands not a word of English, the Reader will have no cause to wonder, if he sometimes meet with *ant* for *and*, *bu* for *but*, *te* for *the*, *is* for *it*, *tit* for *tis*, *wish* for *with*, etc., and oftentimes with false Pointings, words unduly joined, and syllables un-artificially divided at the end of lines, as *Ro-me*, *appropria-te*, and the like. I can assure him, the Correction of the Press cost little less pains than the writing of the Treatise."

In that century a great many English books were printed on the Continent, at Paris, Douai, and elsewhere; and the situation thus candidly explained must have been a common one. A collection of English books printed abroad, which would be interesting for other reasons, might also have an added interest as a repository of comic misprints. But my disease must have brought me very low that I can spend my time thinking of that.

The Bible as Raw Material

MR. GEORGE MOORE'S new novel, *The Brook Kerith,* is a Biblical story. Mr. Moore has adopted the legend which says that Our Lord survived the Crucifixion. He is taken away alive and joins a colony of the Essenes, complications afterwards arising with St. Paul. The book is named after the site of the Essene settlement; Mr. Moore personally toured the Holy Land looking for a really eligible position. The story opens with a description of the boyhood of Joseph of Arimathea: a beginning which at least avoids the reproach of being obvious.

One might almost say that literature about Biblical personages can only hope to be good if its writers either deal with episodes that are not related in the Bible or if they tell the Bible stories from an entirely novel and unconventional point of view. Anatole France's story about Pontius Pilate, *The Procurator of Judaea,* has this last quality, and owes its success mainly to the odd and unexpected angle from which the subject is approached. The unusual angle we may at least expect from Mr. George Moore. Attempts at covering the same ground as the Bible, at amplifying an already fine thing, are almost pre-

168

The Bible as Raw Material

destined to failure. One can understand the temptation. A modern writer comes across a noble story or a fine lyric passage, and thinks, " What a scandal that this should be buried away out of sight in the Old Testament! It is just the theme for me." The lure is so strong that one contemporary poet has attempted, and failed (through not ignominiously), to rewrite David's Lament for Jonathan, and another has endeavoured to adapt the dramatic poem *Job* to the modern stage. It was a lamentable affair, redeemed only from complete inconspicuousness by a highly incongruous chorus inspired by Swinburne and by an arresting entry of Satan with the salutation:

Ho Job!   How goes it?

No modern — but I have not thoroughly ransacked my memory — has really succeeded in rewriting a Bible story. The most striking of recent efforts was Mr. Sturge Moore's *Judith*. Mr. Robert Trevelyan's poem, *The Foolishness of Solomon* (a title that, for some vague reason, I always resent), belonged to the other class of works dealing with Biblical personages (though he brought in a Chinese mandarin as well), but not on the Biblical lines. The most recent effort at elaborate treatment of the New Testament story was, I suppose, Maeterlinck's *Mary Magdalene*. But in spite of its unorthodoxy and the novelty (at least as far as the Bible is con-

169

cerned, for some of it was borrowed from a German) of the incidents, that play scarcely competed, in point of dialogue or dramatic force, with the more old-fashioned narratives of Matthew, Mark, Luke, and John.

Milton is the one English writer who has done anything with Biblical materials on a large scale. It will be observed, however, that in *Paradise Lost* he enormously elaborated the story in Genesis; that his Adam and Eve are somewhat colourless; and that the finest parts of his poem are not directly concerned with "man's first disobedience and the fruit," but deal with regions into which the author of Genesis did not penetrate. In *Samson Agonistes* he did take a story from the Bible and make out of it a work of art equal to almost anything in our language. Byron's *Cain* might mostly have been about Nietzsche for all the connexion it has with the Bible: but it is not very good. Almost every fine subject in the Scriptures must have been attacked at one time or another. There have been a few good short Biblical poems, like Browning's *Saul*. But the only other really reputable Biblical poem on a large scale that I can think of is Charles Wells's *Joseph and His Brethren*, which has strength as a story and some passages of fine imagery. Wells belonged to the generation of Keats and lived on into our own time. He was an engineer, stopped writing when young, and was admired by Rossetti

The Bible as Raw Material

and Swinburne. His poem, however, cannot really be considered such good reading as the Bible account of the same story. One of the episodes that came within his purview, that of Joseph and Potiphar's wife, has been a subject for poets in all ages. The last endeavour that I can recall to make something out of it was a somewhat bejewelled one of Sir Edwin Arnold's. The longest, I should think, is Joshua Sylvester's intolerably tedious series of couplets entitled *The Maiden's Blush*. Why he conferred that title upon such a poem I don't know, unless he was thinking of what might happen to the less robust of his female readers. Those parts of Holy Writ which are of purely historical interest have not been freely drawn on by English writers. I don't remember that much has been done with the Maccabees, and the chronicles of the Kings of Israel, which supplied Racine with a subject for his *Athalie*, have left English writers cold. Jehu drove furiously, Jeroboam the son of Nebat made Israel to sin, and Rehoboam afflicted his people with scorpions instead of whips; but their violence does not seem to fire the poetic imagination as does that of Herod, about whom we know very little more. But Herod, of course, was fond of the Russian ballet; which brings him closer to us.

How to avoid Bad English

GOOD books on the practice of writing are rare. Sir A. Quiller-Couch's *On the Art of Writing* is extraordinarily good. It contains the lectures he delivered at Cambridge just before the war; and even readers who do not desire to write at all will find Sir Arthur's jokes very amusing and his criticisms, general and particular, sound and (what is more unusual) new. He touches a great variety of subjects, though always in some relation to the main theme. He is especially illuminating on the Authorized Version, and on Homer's skill in dealing with the " Primary Difficulty of Verse "— that is to say, the difficulty of filling up the interstices between highly emotional passages without lapsing into dull prosiness. His most diverting chapter is that on what he calls " Jargon," which he distinguishes from Journalese. The distinction he draws may be appreciated if I concoct examples of both commodities. Writing in " Jargon " I might say:

" In the case of Sir Arthur Quiller-Couch I am proud and happy to associate myself in the fullest sense with a work of this useful, elevating, instructive, and educative character."

172

How to avoid Bad English

Writing in Journalese, as he defines it, I might say:

" ' Q.'s brilliant book goes to the root of the matter. It strikes home. He is out to slay the dragons of bad writing. He burns them with the fire of his passion. He lashes them with the scourge of his invective. He tears them to shreds and tatters with the shrapnel of his ridicule. He will not sheathe the sword until . . ."

Yes. . . . The first kind consists of woolly, indefinite words, of redundancies and shapeless prolixities; the man who writes the second is trying to produce what he believes to be " literature " by means of imagery and rhythmical movement. Sir Arthur says that the greatest propagators of Jargon are public bodies, politicians, and so on; but he recognizes that journalists also use it. The two things, in fact, are often seen in one article. I conceive that there might be passages which would fall into either of Sir Arthur's classes. But there is a clear difference between bad sentences produced by an effort to say something and those produced by an effort to say something vividly. All bad writers, however, have common defects, and these are dealt with in other chapters.

Every one who has thought about the art at all has discovered for himself the truths that Sir Arthur

Books in General

tabulates. One must aim at accuracy (a word that covers almost everything that is needful) and at clarity; one must, normally, prefer the concrete to the abstract word, and the short word to the long; and one must avoid the superfluous adjective. How well we know these rules; how certain we are of their validity; how feebly we struggle to obey them! At all times the ready-made sentence, the makeshift epithet, the pot-shot image must have been ready to the hand. In the present age, when we live in a honeycomb of print and begin each day by exposing ourselves, before, during, or after breakfast, to masses of the weakest English we can find, the job of writing well is more difficult than ever. Our fluency is the measure of our accursed memory. We have bales of phrases ready for every experience we describe; our pigeon-holes are stuffed with dead metaphors and bogus synonyms; and we are always ready to say in six words what ought to be said in two. Every time we sit down at a desk or open our lips to speak, the nymphs Jargonia and Journalesia, besieging us as the sylphs besieged St. Anthony, hold out their hands full of glittering treasures which will save us the trouble of thinking. Usually we do not even see them; we find the fatal gifts in our hands and employ them without remembering their origin. And the descent to hell is rapid.

It is good to revise: to correct, to improve, and to delete. Few, even of the most careful writers,
174

How to avoid Bad English

find their proof-sheets free from trite and superfluous words which they would be ashamed to publish.   It is better still to think long before writing,
to make sure that one's thoughts are clear-cut before
one gives them a visible form.   That habit it is
a writer's duty to acquire.   But it does not do to be
incessantly and acutely conscious of the qualities of
good writing and the difficulty of securing them.
That way madness lies.   Sometimes, to a man who
broods overmuch on these things, every phrase will
appear a cliché, and every word a dummy.   " God
help me ! " he will moan, " I have called the sun
' bright ' and the grass ' green ' !   Millions of men
before me have written ' bright sun ' and ' green
grass.'   I know I did not think freshly and inde-
pendently *at* these objects.   I put the adjectives
down mechanically.   I have merely heard that the
grass was green.   Why haven't I looked at it
through my own eyes?   If a real writer looked at
it, I don't for a moment suppose that its greenness
would be the attribute which would impinge most
forcibly upon him.   Very likely it isn't green at all."
This, I say, does not do.   I don't suggest that there
is anything peculiar about grass which should make
a novel statement about it impossible.   In fact,
Swinburne said that grass is hair, and Mr. Chesterton has very probably said that it is red.   I merely
use " green grass " as an example of the sort of
thing that an exaggerated fastidiousness might lead
a man to question in his own work.

Books in General

There remains one property of good prose that no amount of painstaking or instruction can produce. That is rhythm. It is, indeed, remarkable that one of the most elaborate analyses of prose rhythms hitherto made was made by a writer whose own prose is anything but musical. Either Providence has given a man an ear or it has not; if it has not, he will not write great prose. But his prose will be better in proportion as he obeys the principles of good writing as " Q." enunciates them. One suggestion more might be useful for him. That is, that he will be well advised in making his uneuphonious sentences short if he desires his writing to be an efficient instrument of persuasion.

Woodland Creatures

"PARNASSUS in Piccadilly," is the headline I
see in my paper. Follows an account of a
" séance " promoted by Miss Elizabeth Asquith in aid of the Star and Garter Home. Ten or
twelve poets read works of their own to an audience
of four hundred who had paid a guinea apiece. Outside the house a large concourse watched the poets
arrive. There were Mr. Yeats, Sir O. Seaman, Mr.
Hewlett, Sir Henry Newbolt, Mr. Binyon, Mr. de-
la Mare, Mrs. Woods, Mr. Belloc, and Mr. W. H.
Davies, who is described as looking like " one of his
own woodland creatures." I read that one of the
reciters intoned, that another was bluff, and that a
third ought to get somebody else to read for him;
also that Mr. Birrell, the chairman, sat with his
head buried in his hands until the arrival of the
first comic turn, Mr. Belloc's. But I wish I had
been there: for the account does not tell me how it
was really done.

Did the poets sit in the audience and march up
to the platform one by one as their turns came?
Did they stand out of sight, each gliding in singly,
and then retiring into the antral seclusion of the

177

Books in General

wings when ten minutes was up? Or did they rather, as I prefer to think, sit on the platform, the whole dozen of them in a semicircle, listening to, and discreetly applauding, each other's efforts. I am sorry I missed it. Some of them will have been exalted by a sense of the holiness of their work; their eyes will have looked out across the audience with a prophetic and otherworldly fire. Others will have been uneasy and not knowing (unless a table was thoughtfully provided) what to do with their feet. And one or two, I think, will have been preoccupied with the control of their own faces, which, on such an occasion, must have " strained at the leash of dignified deportment."

Why is it that so many people feel awkward when they are present at a public recitation by a poet of his own verse; and why should writers shrink from such recitations? Amusement on such occasions is closely allied to sheepishness: both spring from a feeling of inappropriateness, a sense that " the fitness of things " is being violated. We are accustomed, of course, to the other kind of recitation, the reading by an interpreter who is not a creator, and who is not exposing his heart in public: the prize child and the local elocutionist who declaims Tennyson's *Revenge,* daintily fluttering his fingers in the air when he comes to the part about the pinnace which is like a bird. But our poets themselves have not recited much. It was not always so. " 'Omer
178

Woodland Creatures

smote his bloomin' lyre " in public; he had nowhere
else to smite it, for he (presumably) could not write,
and his audiences could not read. Every composer
of tribal lays, from Tubal-Cain (unless his songs
were *Lieder ohne Wörte*) to the Druidic harpists,
sang his compositions to his admiring fellows without embarrassment; troubadours and mediæval
laureates had no objection at all to public recitation.
Most foreigners, one supposes, do not feel so
strongly as we do about it now; but the timidity of
Englishmen in the matter is very pronounced. I am
sure that nothing short of the needs of a War Fund
would have induced some of the Piccadilly performers to face the ordeal.

It is all a part of our national reserve, that very
reserve which, perhaps, accounts for the greatness
and volume of our poetry. In poetry our feelings
find an outlet. We have the habit of concealing our
finest sentiments and our profoundest emotions.
We don't mind putting them into books and then running round the corner out of sight. But we dislike
unbosoming them *viva voce* in the actual physical
presence of strangers. Our dislike of " scenes "
covers equally the public row in a restaurant and the
public demonstration of our yearnings after virtue
and the stirrings of our hearts when we hear the
nightingale or listen to the Atlantic at night. We
sit bolt upright at concerts; look at pictures with our
mouths set like vices; and observe " Yes, very nice "
as, with wistfulness in our breasts, we stand on a

179

hill and look at a wooded panorama under the moon. The grotesque Englishman who stares at a sunset and then laughs and says it looks like a fried egg is really bolting in terror from the admission that it looks like the flaming ramparts of the world. So, if somebody gets up to recite his most intimate feelings, we feel it as almost an indecency. He is usually bashful about it himself, and unable therefore to recite with that abandonment which will do his poem justice. The audience, at least that part of it which is most intelligent and self-conscious, feels as if it were intruding. It is like eavesdropping or opening a stranger's letters. And everybody is conscious of the national titter in the background. When the authors of Prize Poems at the Universities give the official reading of their verses, their friends invariably assemble to grin in the galleries. Undergraduates have still some naturalness. They titter aloud, but the adult Englishman titters in silence. It is reserve that brings forth the titter and it is still more reserve that suppresses it; just as it is reserve that makes our soldiers sing, not invocations to England, home, or glory, but comic songs about cowardice and death.

The foregoing series of platitudes, slightly varied in accordance with each writer's tastes and talents, is invariably repeated when the character of English people is under discussion. But it may be that, at any rate in our attitude towards poetry, we are

Woodland Creatures

changing. In the last four or five years the habit of public readings has been growing; and some of our poets have grown quite addicted to them. This may be a time of transition: if the enthusiasts for recitation keep at it hard enough, people's constraint may be overcome, and it may be regarded as quite an ordinary and natural thing for a man to stand on a platform and, with all the passion he can release and all the vocal modulation he can command, chant his lyrics to congregations which will yield themselves to him with all the spontaneity, though less than all the gestures and ejaculations, of a Welsh revivalist's converts. It is a commonplace that poetry gains by being spoken; and that if verse were always read and never recited, poets would be in danger of getting out of touch with natural speech-rhythms. We could do with a little less amusement and a little more excitement; and we might as well, if cowardice or a sense of humour are the only things that hold us back, hold and attend public readings until we are as unselfconscious about them as we are about church services or political meetings. The worst of it is that poets do not invariably read well, and that few persons with the taste for standing on a platform and declaiming are competent to take an author's place as reciter of his work. There is such a thing as the inspired reader of other people's verse; but the understanding, the inclination, and the voice cannot be expected to come often together. When the author himself is reciting you can at least be certain that the speaker — unless he is a very " advanced " poet indeed — understands the work which he is repeating. With other performers one always has to take one's chance. From the professional reciter God save us all.

Other People's Books

LIKE most people, I possess a number of books which I have not read. I am not referring to volumes, such as the *Speculum Morale* of Vincent of Beauvais or the commentary of Œcolampadius on St. John's Gospel, which I bought merely because they looked pleasant and which nobody on earth could be expected to read. I mean books in English and of comparatively recent date. There is, for example, Kant's *Critique of Pure Reason,* for which, in a weak moment, I paid some shillings with the feeling that, as a cogitative being, I ought not leave so notable a stone unturned. The feeling passed and never came back. And there is Ranke's *History of the Popes* — up to the present undisturbed by me; there are *The Last Days of Pompeii, Romola, Vittoria,* Carlyle's essays on Burns and Scott, *What Maisie knew, What Katy did,* and dozens of other modern works, some of which, if I live, I shall certainly read, and others of which, I am sure, I shall never begin. But it makes no difference. Whether he has read them or not, a man's own books get, in a manner, stale to him. If a book remains for years unopened on one's shelves it becomes increasingly difficult to read it. Yet if one finds another edition of it in somebody else's

Books in General

house one may fly to it, and, under the same conditions, one may read or re-read almost anything one
finds.

So it is, at the moment, with me. I am in a place
previously unknown to me. It is bestrewn with
books; and, penned to the house by the brilliant summer weather, I have been doing some miscellaneous
reading. For one thing I have gone solidly once
more through Mr. Thomas Hardy's verse. How
extraordinarily good it is! And how remarkably he
has gone on improving, especially as a metrist. But
more than ever, after a heavy dose of these compressed statements of his point of view, one realizes
his determined and unmitigated gloom. It is at its
densest in *Wessex Poems,* and in places one laughs
outright at it. He illustrated the book himself, his
drawing is naïve, and the sketch of two floors of a
church, the pews (and two lovers) above, and the
skulls and cross-bones below, has an " I *will* be grim
at all costs " air about it that robs it of all its horror.
The story attached is a neat one. The man is a con-
sumptive about to die; he asks the woman if she
loves him? She falsely says " Yes " in order to
brighten his last hours. He dies, and her life is
ever after blighted because she cannot reconcile herself to a Universe in which the telling of such lies is
a moral obligation. There is another small drama
in which a woman, maltreated by her husband, dies,
telling her old lover that she wishes she had married

Other People's Books

him and that her child could have been his child, and asking him to see that the brutal husband does not ill-treat the child. The brutal husband remarries and does ill-treat the child. One day he finds the lover mourning on the dead wife's grave, and demands by what right he is there. The lover, remembering the death-bed remark and suddenly seeing a chance of saving the child, says that he has every right to be there as he was really the father of the child. His supposed offspring is then left on his doorstep, to be looked after carefully, and he spends his time wondering whether he was justified in telling, etc. Probably these stories, if expanded into novels, might convince; as narrative poems they do not; and when they are squeezed into the brief compass of the *Satires of Circumstance* they are grotesquely Life as Thomas Hardy makes it and not Life as Thomas Hardy sees it.

It is a little bold in these days to admit that one hasn't read the whole of Mr. Conrad's works, but until this week I had never laid hands on *Almayer's Folly*. It was his first book. In his *Reminiscences* he gives an account of how it was begun, in a Pimlico lodging-house, when he was a sea captain and carried about the ocean for five years until (when he was thirty-five) he finished it. When, half-done and laid by, it was yellowing and mouldering, he showed it to his first reader, a Cambridge man going to Australia for his health, and asked him if it was worth com-

185

pleting. The passenger, with a nice economy of words, answered " Distinctly," and Captain Conrad was thus encouraged to proceed. I had read all this before, and also the novelist's statement that before this he had not attempted literature and had hardly ever written even a letter — though I suppose there must have been an occasional entry in a log. I have certainly been surprised by the craftsmanship of *Almayer's Folly*. Not only is the structure good, but the writing, except in one or two places, is astonishingly finished, accurate, and restrained. It is absurdly unlike a first book. Its weakness, as it appears to me, lies in the dullness of the principal character. It is difficult to keep up one's interest in a person whose main characteristic is his impotence. But it doesn't matter so much here as it might, for the subsidiary story of Dain and Nina is very fascinating, and the real hero, after all, is none of the people, white or Malay, but the Bornean river (its topography is not always clear to me) on whose overgrown banks they all live and the changes of which, night and day, are described with marvellous eloquence and certainty.

Peacock

FINALLY, after various minor excursions, I have settled down to the works of Thomas Love Peacock, of whom I had read nothing before except some poems. Why? I don't know, but I think his name has vaguely repelled me. Anyhow, I am thankful now that I have been able to come fresh to Peacock's novels. He has a few devotees, but it is surprising that so admirable a writer is not more read. *Nightmare Abbey* and *Headlong Hall* are not great masterpieces, but they are certainly small masterpieces. They belong to the class of intellectual comedy to which *Candide,* and, in some measure, *Rasselas* belong; in fact, they must certainly have been modelled on *Candide.* They are burlesques of oneself and one's friends, and every other discussing, theorizing person and his friends. Charlatans of all kinds, literary, political, eccelesiastical, and scientific, and philosophers of all kinds from the man who believes that upward progress is inevitable to the man who believes that downward progress is undeniable, from the secret revolutionary conspirator to the professional sceptic; he gets them all in, quintessentializes their doctrines into exquisitely flowing prose, and knocks their heads together with charming ruthlessness. Any extract will illustrate the flow of his dialogue:

Books in General

"'The anatomy of the human stomach,' said Mr. Escot, ' and the formation of the teeth, clearly place man in the class of fungivorous animals.'

"'Many anatomists,' said Mr. Foster, 'are of a different opinion, and agree in discerning the characteristics of the carnivorous classes.'

"'I am no anatomist,' said Mr. Jenkinson, ' and cannot decide where doctors disagree; in the meantime, I conclude that man is omnivorous, and on that conclusion I act.'

"'Your conclusion is truly orthodox,' said the Reverend Doctor Gaster; ' indeed, the loaves and fishes are typical of a mixed diet, and the practice of the Church in all ages shows ——'

"'That it never loses sight of the loaves and fishes,' said Mr. Escot."

If loud asseveration on my part sends to Peacock a few people who have not tried him before, I shall feel that the recent rain has not descended in vain.

Wordsworth's Personal Dullness

THE Strange Case of William Wordsworth is to me of perennial interest, and I have just emerged from several days' burrowing under Professor C. G. Harper's two enormous volumes entitled *William Wordsworth, His Life, Works, and Influence.* It is a conscientious and valuable piece of work, very fully documented, and containing much out-of-the-way information and a great deal of sensible, if not always illustrious, criticism. The information may perhaps be a little too ample for the weaker brethren. The map (showing lakes, mountain ranges (brown) and so on) of Wordsworth's country with which we open gives the clue to Professor Harper's exhaustive method. Every procurable date of Wordsworth's continental programme is copied out; and we are even supplied with the winter and summer timetables of the Grammar School at Hawkshead which he attended and at which (as Professor Harper rather sententiously observes) an education different in kind, but perhaps not inferior in quality, to that supplied by Eton was bestowed upon him. New light is thrown on certain incidents in his career; his " circle " is

Books in General

elaborately described; and a very charming picture is given of his sister Dorothy. But the old problem of Wordsworth's defects remains much where it did.

It is a commonplace that Wordsworth is the most uneven of great poets. Every textbook writer tells one that when he was inspired he was a giant, that when he was not he wrote maundering doggerel, and that he himself never knew when he was and when he was not at his best. *The Idiot Boy* has been held up to the ridicule of generations — beyond its deserts perhaps. The point was most forcibly put by J. K. Stephen when he wrote a parody of Wordsworth's " Two voices are there," saying that one of the voices was that of the sea, etc., and the other that of " an old half-witted sheep." But a thing less frequently faced, and never, as far as I know, properly explained, is his personal lack of attractiveness. Flippant persons may be met who dismiss him as " a pompous old dullard "; but, generally speaking, whenever one hears such a remark it comes from some one who openly confesses that he cannot stand Wordsworth's poetry at any price, and that he has very seldom attempted to read it. The people who are in difficulties are those (and I am among them) who agree without qualification that Wordsworth is our greatest poet since Milton, but who cannot sincerely say that they are drawn towards him as a man. If they — any one who does not feel like this is happy and I do not speak

for him — pretend to be fond of him their pretence
is glaring. If they do not stick up for him they
feel that they are being faithless to a poet who still
stands in need of all the propagandists he can get.
It is not easy to face the truth about him even in the
solitude of one's own chamber. But, by heaven,
he *is* a dull man!

" There was a boy " (as Wordsworth would himself begin) who at one time used nightly to dine in
hall under a large oil-painting of the poet. In this
painting Wordsworth was represented sitting on a
rock against a landscape background which was an
agreeable and symbolical blend of wildness and tran-
quillity. The poet was clad in broadcloth; he held
a book in his hand; his face was smooth and pink;
and his mild eye surveyed the spectator as though
the latter were a lamb about to receive a pat of the
hand and his blessing. There he sat, meditative and
benevolent, while the soup gave place to the fish
and the fish to the beef; and when one had drained
off the last dregs of one's beer one went off still
conscious of that meditative and benevolent eye.
It became almost maddening. Every other great
English poet had something fascinating about him.
Even Milton, in spite of certain unsociable qualities,
had a certain attractive force, a touch of the virulent,
and the scars of suffering. But this Wordsworth!
His genuine philanthropy was unquestionable. His
portrait might, one thought, be that of a pioneer of

Books in General

the Anti-Slave Trade Agitation, or an inventor of
Sunday Schools, or an endower of Bands of Hope.
But not a poet; oh, not a poet!

So it is with all his portraits. Professor Harper
gives a selection of them. Always the sage is a
bland and upright man; the *mens conscia recti* typi-
fied. But never a sign of eloquence or fire; of the
magnificent oratory of his great passages, of the
music and profound tenderness which are so profuse
in his poetry. Not a sign of stress; not a mark of
any but the most complacent vicarage thought; no
passion, no enthusiasm, no challenge, and no response. It is not to be explained away, as Professor
Harper attempts to explain it away, by saying that
the myth of " Daddy Wordsworth " (as FitzGerald
called him) is based on a disproportionate view of
his life. Professor Harper thinks that far too little
attention has been paid to his early revolutionary
period, when the ideals of the French Revolution
gripped him, and far too much to his later period
of orthodoxy and respectability. Professor Harper
himself attempts to redress the balance. He gives
as full an account as he can of the earlier Wordsworth and of his relations with Revolutionary
France. But, as Wordsworth's French friends
would have said (provided they were not ashamed
of using such a worn-out tag) *plus ça change plus
c'est la même chose*. The early Wordsworth may
have been a different being; but Professor Harper
192

Wordsworth's Personal Dullness

certainly does not prove that he was. From birth
to death in this biography he appears as the same
high-minded, staid, sober, solemn monument. He
joined in the Revolution not so much a " kid-glove
revolutionary " as a woollen-glove and warm com-
forter revolutionary. Had he stayed in France he
might have made even the Terror respectable.

On myself and on others Wordsworth's portraits
and his biographies always leave this sort of impression: the impression of an old bore to whom one
would not be rude simply and solely because one
would not willingly hurt the feelings of a person so
worthy. And then one goes back to his poetry —
and his prose — and hears a voice of almost unsurpassed grandeur speaking the deepest of one's un-
expressed thoughts, appealing to and drawing out
all the divinest powers in man's nature. Of his
greatness surely no rational and unbiassed being
could entertain the slightest doubt. He is not so
popular or so frequently read as some poets, and that
is not difficult to explain. His absence of humour,
or an equivalent vivacity, is not in itself an explanation; but the accompanying general absence of any
luxurious appeal to the senses is. He speaks direct
to the labouring intellect and the sensitive heart;
and the enjoyment of him, if great, is usually enjoyment of the austerer kind, like mountain-climbing.
There is nothing soft or enervating or luxurious
which can make reading him an æsthetic debauch.

He does not often sing to a tune which gives one pleasure even if one does not attend to the words. Without being in the least obscure he demands an effort from the reader parallel to his own. That, at least as much as the tediousness of many of his writings (and his irritating classification of them), is the reason of his comparative lack of popularity. But . . .

Henry James's Obscurity

HENRY JAMES'S last work was his essay on Rupert Brooke, written as an introduction to *Letters from America.* Mr. James's essay is a personal appreciation, and not in any way a biographical memoir. Such a memoir, by another hand, will follow. Mr. James left unfinished two novels, and a third volume of the series begun with *A Small Boy and Others* and *Notes of a Son and Brother.*

Presumably the public (which might well make a start with the short stories of which Mr. Secker has already published eight half-crown volumes, very pleasant to the eye) will at last begin to buy James's novels. They have certainly not bought them in the past. He was, in critical circles, almost universally recognized as one of the three or four greatest of English writers living a week ago. But some of his books had not even gone into a second edition. He was intermittently talked about in the Press. Fifteen years or so ago he had a boom of the sort; then there was a period of comparative newspaper obscurity; in the last three or four years he suddenly and silently, like a star appearing from behind a cloud, took his unchallenged

place in the firmament as one of the established
great. But he was not widely read. *Daisy Miller,*
ever so many years ago, had a fairly general success; *The Golden Bowl,* also, I should think, sold
well. But many people who paid lip homage to
him were very unfamiliar with his work.

In no case would a man with his interests, his
approach, his subtlety and avoidance of the grosser
excitements, his restraint and delicacy, have sold by
the hundred thousand. But his appeal was still further limited by the legend of his style. I remember
reading an old novel written in the days when Robert Browning was an Incomprehensible studied by a
Cult. The heroine of it gave herself away rather
by remarking, " Oh, Mr. Browning! I've never
been able to understand a single thing that he has
written. That is why I have never tried." One
feels that there were persons who were in the same
position as towards Henry James. They had
heard that he was a hard nut to crack; they had
seen perhaps — it was always a great temptation
to a reviewer to extract — specimens of his more
elaborate discursions, complicated arabesques of
sentences, parenthesis after parenthesis wandering
from comma to comma like barbed wire tangled
around its supports. And they thought therefore
that he was an obscure eclectic as difficult as Jacob
Behmen or Swedenborg and lacking their excuse of
religious inspiration. Certainly he was sometimes

196

Henry James's Obscurity

difficult. But it was a unique kind of obscurity. There is an obscurity produced when a man, eagerly tumbling along an argument, writes down only a sort of fitful shorthand, a language which leaves things out and which resembles the stray pieces of disconnected paper in gutter or hedge which merely indicate the course that the runner has taken. There is another and commoner kind of obscurity of speech which derives from mistiness of mind; for a man cannot write clearly down what he does not clearly think. And there is a kind of obscurity which is produced by mere inaptitude for writing: the awkwardness of the cow handling a rifle. James's obscurity was the direct product of his passion for clarity. He detested the slipshod sentence which, compact as it may look as a piece of grammar, is a mere pot-shot as a piece of representation. He wanted to make no statement which did not embody precisely what he wanted to say; what, that is to say, he saw as Truth. He would have taken, for example, that last sentence of mine and, endeavouring to give it a more exact shape, have made of it something like the following:

" He wanted, when, that is, he experienced anything so definite or, shall we put it, so positively energetic, as a want, to make no statement, none at any rate which might be taken by even the least perceptive of his hearers as a *delivered*, and, as it were, final testimony of his reaction to things as he saw

197

them, which did not precisely embody what he
wanted (when, once more, he coherently desired
anything, as we have it, " higher " than the elemen-
tary physical) to say; what, that is to say, he saw,
at the moment of speech, be it understood, for the
eye of the watcher changes, as what, in the absence
of a happier name, it has pleased us to ennoble with
the majestic name of Truth."

I don't suggest that I myself have added anything
to my own sentence by this addition of the pomp
and circumstance of parenthesis and circumlocution.
I have merely turned a short platitude into a long
one.   But it may serve to show the method by which
Henry James arrived at his more tortuous pages.
The method has its disadvantages.   The man who
employs it is sometimes like a man working with a
pickaxe in a cave.   The more he digs away the
larger the unattacked expanse which invites his
strength; or, as one might say, the bigger the hole
he is in.   But when this method is employed by a
man with the analytical powers, the sensitiveness to
fine shades, material and spiritual, of Henry James,
the result is a " product " (the kind of word that
James would always have put in actual or implied
inverted commas) which never stales and from
which one gets more and more enjoyment each time
one reads.   In the last resort novels live by the
richness of their detail; and James's detail is exquisite and inexhaustible.

198

Henry James's Obscurity

Few modern writers have exercised so strong an influence over those who have surrendered themselves to him. He is, I should say, more infectious than any writer since (what a strange collocation!) Lord Macaulay. A man with a formed style can usually read and enjoy Carlyle, Jeremy Taylor, de Quincey, or George Meredith without showing the least tendency (unless deliberate) to imitate them. But when one has (I don't speak only for myself) been reading James one finds for a time that one is tempted to write even one's private letters in a style which shows plainly that one has set him as a seal upon one's arm. Even now, when I am merely thinking about him, I feel the pressure of that stern artistic conscience, and can only with an effort resist the demand that I should guard myself here, qualify myself here, and elucidate myself there. He was irresistible, like one of those stammerers or persons with other attractive or unattractive vocal idiosyncrasies whom one cannot help imitating when one is with them. A person of any force gets through this and the permanent effect of a subjugation to James was always good. A too marked echo of him would be painful: but his example was salutary. It may be possible to grumble with him for this and that. He did write mainly about persons with incomes (though these also are God's creatures); he did occasionally behave (as Mr. Wells very wittily put it) like a hippopotamus picking up a pea; and he did annoy some enthusiasts by refusing to place his pen habitually at the service of the Great Forces of Our Time and other things whose capital importance is of custom indicated by capital letters. But in an age of sloppy writing he stood for accuracy of craftmanship; and even men whose subjects are Invisible Exports of the Parthenogenesis of Plants might learn from him how to use to more advantage their intellects and their pens.

The "Ring" in the Bookselling Trade

A BIBLIOPHILE writes the following complaint: " At the recent sale of Swinburne's library, certain lots, chiefly signed presentation copies, fetched extravagantly high prices. But the outsider is generally puzzled at the extreme variation in the prices, a variation which passing fashions in taste do not explain. There is an explanation, as one would-be purchaser was made somewhat rudely aware. He wanted a book by a modern poet, a poet of delicate talent and little recognition; and he asked a bookseller to bid for the lot. He was willing to spend between ten and thirteen shillings on it. The agent who was to bid arrived late, and another bookseller bought the lot for five shillings. So the would-be purchaser asked his bookseller to approach the man who had bought the lot, and find out if he would sell it. The book was cheap at five and would be rather dear at ten shillings. When approached, the purchaser informed his colleague that ' he had had to pay a good deal more for the lot than the price given in the rooms, and that he could not part with it for less than eighteen shillings.' Such are the blessings of the ' ring ' at Sotheby's.

Books in General

"The ring consists of some of the largest and best-known members of the bookselling trade — all honest men — and their plan is this: they never bid against each other, except for show; lots go at small prices, thus robbing owners and executors of their right profit; and subsequently these cheap lots are put up again and resold among the members of the ring. The auctioneers can, of course, do nothing to stop the practice — and it is as legal as it is dishonourable. At times an outsider with a big banking account gives the ring a good deal of trouble; but it has survived all private attacks, and is likely to — though a private buyer with a confident manner and a quick power of decision can occasionally get a great deal of amusement by running lots up, and so forcing the ring to pay exorbitant prices for things they do not want."

It is true. There exists among the second-hand booksellers precisely such a ring as gave rise to so much discussion a few years ago when the scandal of the art-dealers' "knock-out" was widely discussed. For some time I myself have been trying to get information about it. But it is not easy. You can find out from booksellers who are not in the ring (few of these lone wolves are important) who the booksellers are who are in the ring, but that is about all. But the method is simple. The attendance at book sales is not large. Private collectors are lazy people; it is not now fashionable —

The "Ring" in the Bookselling Trade

as it was in the Duke of Roxburghe's day — for the Old Nobility to crowd the salerooms, bidding desperately amid groans of anguish and cheers of triumph. The result is that very often one will attend a sale and be the only private person there, and it is a matter of chance (especially when the sale is a comparatively small one) whether any one at all is there except the members of the ring. The ring, *pro forma,* will run a book up to about a third of its value and leave it at that. At the close of the proceedings its members will adjourn somewhere — I don't know where, but let us say a back room in the Charing Cross Road — and hold a " knock-out " auction of the books they have bought. The difference between the sums paid here and the sums paid at Sotheby's or Hodgson's will be pooled and divided, so as to equalize the spoil; and the owners of the libraries sold will have got only, perhaps, a half of what they really ought to have got considering the prices that the ultimate purchasers are willing to pay.

But I don't see what is to be done about it. As my correspondent remarks, the auctioneers can't stop it. They also must suffer as their work is done on a commission basis. It must not be assumed that all the booksellers like the system, but the minority cannot help themselves. I remember that one very well known bookseller, now dead, tried for several years to keep out of it; but in the end, by

Books in General

co-ordinated bidding against him, he was forced in. There the thing is; the dealers find it profitable; it is not easy to keep out of it unless you are a prince of the trade, with rich customers and great resources, or a person with special knowledge who is after a special kind of book and will be let alone; and there is no short cut to reform. How can Parliament interfere? If one dealer who buys a book can sell it to another after the sale, how can six or a dozen dealers be prevented from exchanging their purchases similarly. It would be all very well to make the "knock-out" illegal, but how many does it take to make a ring and how many detectives could be spared? The only conceivable remedy is for persons who habitually buy old books to make a point (when the war is over and they are released from their present occupations) of turning up at the salerooms and bidding against the pros. Even at that the remedy would only be efficacious as long as it was actively applied. It might be worth a guinea a box, but you would have to take a box every day; there would be no permanent cure. Directly the strangers slacked off again the ring and the "knock-out" would revive, and my unfortunate friend (for I presume that the disconsolate buyer he refers to is himself) would have once more to pay for his books much more than the price recorded at the rooms. "There is no cure for this disease," as Mr. Belloc's poem puts it, unless auction-frequenting again becomes a popular form of amusement.

204

The "Ring" in the Bookselling Trade

But, if I may digress, I must say that, for persons of a bookish turn of mind, there is nothing more amusing than an occasional visit to Wellington Street or Chancery Lane. I shouldn't care to do it every day; the combined mustiness of books and booksellers is a bit overpowering. But is is exciting to bid occasionally, and the books that come into the London auction-rooms are of such quality that sometimes you might almost as well go to Sotheby's as to the Exhibition Rooms (now shut up so as to pay for two minutes of the war) of the British Museum. The bindings that great collectors put on their books are in themselves wonderful. And the booksellers, rich and poor, glossy and seedy, as they nod to the rostrum and paw the goods, are a sight to which only Balzac could do justice. They all wear looks of settled gloom as though they were on the verge of bankruptcy; they all (if one speaks to them) swear that " it is impossible to get anything to-day as everything is going so dear "; and they all have a sovereign indifference to everything but the commercial value of the books they deal in. I say all: there are exceptions; but the crowd as a whole is utterly depressed and completely free from the remotest concern with literature. But possibly when they get in that back room somewhere and assess the margin between what executors have got for books and what they ought to have got for them, their morose countenances may brighten. For all I know, every " knock-out " auction may end with

Books in General

the circulation of the punch-bowl, jolly songs, and toasts to the damnation of all the idiots who waste their money on rotten old books unfit to read and thereby keep in affluence a set of honest men who read the *Daily Mail* in the morning and never a line for the rest of the day.

Music-Hall Songs

MR. WILLIAM ARCHER contributes to the *Fortnightly* an attack on the music-hall. He says that it is the home of vulgarity and inanity; that the audiences, as a rule, would enjoy much better stuff than they are given; and that " the music-hall seems to have killed a genuine vein of lyric faculty in the English people." With all that I don't think that any one but a poseur could disagree. Mr. Archer makes an extraordinary slip when he puts forward *Sally in our Alley* as a folk-product of which neither the composer nor the author is known to fame: both words and music being by Henry Carey, who was scarcely an obscure person in his day and is not entirely forgotten now. He concludes, too, with a somewhat vague suggestion of a remedy which has no bearing whatever upon the improvement of music-hall songs, and which one suspects to spring from his perennial desire to induce the public to go and see Ibsen. But his case as a whole is irrefutable. The nation's songs since the industrial revolution have been immeasurably worse than at any other time in its history. They are almost all commercial products manufactured by half-wits.

Books in General

Mr. Archer's case being so sound, it is all the more a pity that he overdoes it. It is true that almost all these songs are vile rubbish, and that the songs of the *Villikins and his Dinah* and *Champagne Charlie* periods were even more fatuous than those of the present day. But it is exaggeration to say that

" what is certain is that the whole music-hall movement has produced not one — literally not one — piece of verse that can rank as poetry of the humblest type, or even as a really clever bit of comic rhyming,"

for such songs turn up fairly frequently. Possibly Mr. Archer's horror of the " red-nosed comedian " prevents him from ever listening to his words: certainly one gets from Mr. Archer's article the impression that the critic is only acquainted with a few of the most famous of music-halls songs. But although I heartily support his general case and would willingly consent to the execution of all music-hall managers and versifiers and most music-hall artists, I must protest that " really clever bits of comic rhyming " do turn up occasionally.

I wish I had a better verbal memory. But I can at least refer Mr. Archer to a few songs of which, if he cares to spend a month in the Museum with old volumes of Francis, Day and Hunter's song-books and other collections, he can find the full

Music-Hall Songs

words. For instance, there is Mr. Harry Lauder's *It's Nice to get up in the Morning*. As I remember them (and here and elsewhere I don't guarantee that my quotations are literally accurate) the words of the chorus are:

Oh, it's nice to get up in the morning when the sun begins to shine,
At four or five or six o'clock in the good old summer time;
But when the snow is falling, and it's murky overhead,
It's nice to get up in the morning — but it's nicer to stay in bed.

Of course the tune helped it. But it is quite well turned and it springs clean out of popular experience. It is folk-poetry even if the folk didn't write it. It is not the folk-poetry of the seventeenth century, but it is distinctly the folk-poetry of modern commercial and urban England. *We sat upon the Baby on the Shore* I'm not sure about; it didn't, I suspect, have a music-hall origin, though I do not know. But *A Little Bit off the Top* was quite comic in places; so were *The Four Horse Charabanc, Right in the Middle of the Road, Whitewash,* and *'E dunno where 'e are.* I wish I could recall the words of the song which had a chorus beginning:

More work for the undertaker,
Another little job for the tombstone-maker;

209

but even that high-spirited couplet shows their quality. These mock-tragic songs are often quite good. The best known was *His Day's Work was done,* which was undeniably a comic conception well carried out. Did Mr. Archer ever hear *If it wasn't for the Houses in Between?* The one fragment that sticks in my mind both dates it and shows that it was a " clever bit of comic rhyming ":

> *If the weather had been finer*
> *You'd have seen the war in China —*
> *If it wasn't for the Houses in Between.*

And what about *Waiting at the Church?* —

> *There was I waiting at the church,*
> *Waiting at the church.*
> *When I found he'd left me in the lurch,*
> *Lor', how it did upset me!*
> *Then he sent me round a little note,*
> *Just a little note,*
> *This is what he wrote:*
> *Can't get away to marry you to-day —*
> *My wife won't let me."*

That seems to me a well-calculated chorus, and the clinch of the last two lines couldn't be beaten. But perhaps the austere Mr. Archer would think it debasing on the grounds that it led the audience to think lightly of bigamy.

Music-Hall Songs

Bigamy is one of the chief comic-song subjects. Vermin in one's bed, drunkenness, and the food in boarding-houses are the others. The " booze " songs are not, as a rule, as good as they should be. The only one I remember that was at all neat ran *something* like:

> *First she had some marmalade,*
> *And then she had some jam,*
> *Then some dozen of oysters*
> *And then a plate of ham,*
> *A lobster and a crab or two*
> *And a pint of bottled beer,*
> *A little gin hot to settle the lot*
> *— And that's what made her queer.*

I certainly don't suggest that any of the songs I have quoted — and I'm certain that consultation with a few expert friends, now in Flanders, would bring better ones to light — are masterpieces. But I do think they are quite comic verse, and that if all music-hall songs were as well turned there would not be much ground for complaint. One does, that is, laugh *occasionally* at a music-hall, in spite of Mr. Archer. But, unhappily, of ninety-nine songs out of a hundred the words are too abysmal for anything, and the serious ones are almost invariably imbecile. I wonder, by the way, whether the music-hall authorities ever try to induce competent comic rhymers, known in other spheres, to turn out songs

211

Books in General

for them? Probably not; they think the words
don't matter. That they are mistaken (though the
tunes count for most) is shown by the way that a
song with good words succeeds with the audience.
Even one ingenious line will often bring the house
down. I remember the old song *I can't change it.*
There was a stanza about a bride who appalled
her bridegroom by taking herself to pieces, remov-
ing a wig, a glass eye, a wooden arm, two wooden
legs, etc. In the chorus the narrator suddenly described her as " 'Arf a woman and 'arf a tree," and
this admirable if unrefined trope was the most successful thing of the year. But as I say, I largely
agree with Mr. Archer. If only they would let me
smoke in theatres I would never go near a music-
hall again until the programmes were improved, and
I imagine many other people are in the same boat.

More Music-Hall Songs

HOW little do we know the consequences of our acts. " I say there is not a red Indian, hunting by Lake Winnipic, can quarrel with his squaw, but the whole world must smart for it: will not the price of beaver rise? It is a mathematical fact that the casting of this pebble from my hand alters the centre of gravity of the Universe." That was Carlyle's way of putting it. Somebody wrote a book of theatrical reminiscences: the book set Mr. William Archer pondering on the fatuity of music-halls; Mr. Archer's article made me try to remember comic fragments of music-hall songs; and my observations would appear, judging from the quantities of correspondence they have produced, to have tempted whole families to spend their evenings trying to recall the popular choruses of their youth.

Numbers of them seem to have better memories than mine. Whole verses of *More Work for the Undertaker* (I think it was Mr. Dunville's song) reach me. The scheme may be illustrated by one stanza:

Sammy Snoozer laboured on the railway;
His work he was very clever at!

Books in General

Sammy one day was a-polishing the metals
With a lump of mouldy fat.
Up come a runaway engine,
Sammy stood upon the track;
He held out his arms, for he firmly believed
He could push that locomotive back.
                    (The drum: *Boom! !*)

(Chorus)
More work for the undertaker,
Another little job for the tombstone-maker;
At the local cemetery they've
Been very very busy with a brand-new grave,
For Snoozer's
Snuffed it!

I am afraid that I should have to grant Mr.
Archer the verse: the second line, especially, cannot
be called a model of good craftsmanship. But the
chorus is very neat. It was varied with each verse.
Another correspondent's specimen finishes with
" For Frederick's fragments."

I must bow to the correspondent who suggests
that the success of the song about the bride with
artificial limbs was at least as much due to lines
he quotes as it was to " 'Arf a woman and 'arf a
tree." His lines are:

I can't change her!
No matter how I try,

More Music-Hall Songs

But I'll chop her up for firewood
In the sweet by-and-by.

An equally impolite chorus is that of Herbert Campbell's *'Blige a Lady* which another correspondent sends. The conductor, on a rainy day, asked the inside males to give up a seat to a lady and go outside, and the reply was on the lines of

Said I, " Old chap, she may have my lap,
But I don't get wet for her."

That is very typical music-hall; and it will be observed that it gets its effect by sticking close, as Wordsworth advised, to the natural phraseology and sequence of everyday speech.

Mr. Albert Chevalier, I admit, I did not mention, He has not been primarily a music-hall artist, and Mr. Archer himself made an exception of his songs. Some of Mr. Gus Elen's certainly might be quoted: e. g. *'E dunno where 'e are* and *What's the Use of looking out for Work?* I am afraid that I am not sufficiently well informed to answer questions as to the sources of supply of modern music-hall songs. The only thing I have observed is that large numbers of the worst ones are composed by persons whose names suggest that the use of the English language is with them rather an acquired than an inherited characteristic. How far the practice prevails of a particular star employing a tame author to write the words of all his songs for him I do not know. I have never consciously met a writer of music-hall songs, though I did know one man who made two attempts to produce what he thought the right sort of commodity. He sent them to an entrepreneur, but all his wit was wasted. The chorus of one song mentioned a well-known and much-advertised comestible: this wouldn't do, as all the vendors of similar articles would be jealous and, possibly, refuse to advertise any more on the programme. In the other song the author had had the misfortune to hit upon an idea which had been used before. His refrain was:

And when the pie was opened
The birds began to sing.

But there was an old song with the same tail to it. It was a song about a pigeon-pie which was no better than it should be. This reminds me that in tabulating favourite music-hall subjects one should certainly have mentioned bad smells. Throughout history any reference to unpleasant smells has moved the Englishman to roars of laughter. Perhaps it is because we so thoroughly dislike them. I don't think that these odours take all nations in quite the same way: but travellers on the Continent are sometimes tempted to think that most nations do not notice them so much as we do.

More Music-Hall Songs

The music-hall versifier, usually feeble when funny, is certainly at his worst when serious. Such of the war-songs as I have heard are dreadful. Perhaps those I have not heard are better. Early in the war I was looking into a music-shop window in Upper Shaftesbury Avenue and saw two typical titles. One was *Only a Bit of Khaki that Daddy wore at Mons*, and the other was *The Little Irish Red Cross Nurse*. I did not dare to buy them, but I could not help admiring the ingenuity of the author of the second who had managed to work the perennial Irish Girl theme so neatly into the new subject. All music-hall poets seem to be obsessed by Irish girls. They will even work them into translations of foreign songs which do not mention them. Five or six years ago a German music-hall song which had nothing whatever to do with Irish girls was imported and became very popular here. The ideas of the original were largely preserved, but an Irish girl had to be stuck in. But *quo, Musa, tendis?* If I go on like this I shall end by agreeing with Mr. Archer.

Utopias

I SAW recently a very entertaining article by Mr. Walter Lippman in the *New Republic* on the subject of Utopias. Mr. Lippman raised the question of why it was Utopias had gone out of fashion. Since Mr. Wells wrote his *Modern Utopia* no one has had a shot.

It is, of course, not the longest period in human history which has gone without a new Utopia. As far as I know, nothing of the sort was constructed between the time of Plato and that of Sir Thomas More. Reasons might, no doubt, be discovered for this long lapse. The Romans were too realistic to bother about such things, and in the Middle Ages the only people who could write were priests, and they probably did not dare outline any other perfect society than that of the New Jerusalem. In fact, Utopias of any merit have until recently always been produced at long intervals: with the exception of Bacon's *New Atlantis* and Campanella's *City of the Sun,* which were, I think, published in the same year. The nineteenth century must have produced more imaginary states of this kind than all its predecessors put together. And if we stop constructing Utopias, this will happen not because we have ceased to

Utopias

hanker after them, but because the complexities of civilization have become too unmanageable to handle. When the structures of society and industry were comparatively simple, a man could invent an ideal state which would not look too far removed from the states he knew. We can still go on dreaming of little paradises, such as that in Morris's *News from Nowhere;* but what it is difficult to do is to describe fully an imaginary community which is world-wide, or, at any rate, in contact with the whole world, which has to face the problems of race, and which has to take over from existing civilization our highly developed methods of manufacture and distribution of labour. Mr. Wells did try to depict a state that might grow out of the existing order; but his picture is notably less complete than those of older writers. He could only hope to produce his effect by giving us a series of cinema glimpses of various aspects of life. Personally, I doubt whether any one else will even attempt the job.

One could wish that somebody would make a thorough study of the principal Utopias that the mind of man has conceived. Such a study would offer many interesting paths to research. We might find out, for example, to how great an extent the Utopians of various ages and nations have been influenced (as Plato was conspicuously influenced) by the transient conditions of their own time. For instance, the great variety of opinion which Utopians

Books in General

have held with regard to the precious metals would be worth examination. Some have held them in great respect; others have vindictively suggested that they should be put to the basest possible uses. Again, how far has each writer of this kind been influenced by his predecessor? It can scarcely be supposed, for instance, that Campanella did not lift his communistic ideas bodily from Plato, or that Mr. Wells's class of Samurai owed nothing to the same inspiration. Sometimes one sees a quite minor and obviously personal idea lifted clean or adapted with slight alterations which make it all the more curious. For example, in More's *Utopia* brides and bridegrooms before marriage always inspected each other in a state of nature. It is to be presumed that More had some peculiar crank on this subject; for he mentions the possibility of concealing deformities as though it were a common practice that should certainly be guarded against by law. When we get to Bacon we find this odd idea copied, with the difference that it is now the friends of the respective parties that make the examination.

The endless queer details in Utopias would in themselves make such a study amusing. Plato's passion to secure that no mother should know her own child; the preposterously exact account of the amount of money subscribed towards the foundation of the new state in Theodor Hertzka's *Freeland;* the wonderful battle between the fleets of, if I re-

Utopias

member rightly, Abyssinia and Europe in the same book; the trains going two hundred miles an hour, so smoothly that people played billiards on them, in Mr. Wells's New World. I remember another Utopia, an obscure eighteenth-century one, in which persons who had committed murders were given the choice of being executed in honour or surviving in disgrace. If they chose death they were led to the scaffold amid universal applause, their names were inscribed upon rolls of honour, and their relatives were given fat jobs. Then, again, one could have a quite interesting chapter on the various literary devices by which authors have precipitated readers into their supposititious communities. More's introduction — with the bronzed and bearded seaman who went out with the companions of Columbus and was stranded on an unknown island — is as charming as any. Later dodges have been more far-fetched. Mr. Wells's transferment to the twin-world of this one is very subtle; Edward Bellamy made his hero wake up after centuries in a room where he asked for Edith (his old fiancée) and was conveniently answered by another lady of the same name. I say nothing of the books which lie on the outskirts of Utopian literature, such as various grotesque Utopias and anti-Utopias and books like Lord Lytton's *The Coming Race* and W. H. Hudson's *The Crystal Age,* which last is, I believe, the only book on record which purports to have been written by a man who dies in the last chapter and describes

Books in General

his own demise. And the practical attempts to set up working ideal communities — such as the Oneida community which developed into a prosperous " Mfg. Coy."— are another pleasant by-way.

I think that with all the peculiarities of time and place, all the eccentricities of personal taste, and all the genuine varieties of ideals allowed for, a student of Comparative Utopianism would probably find that there was a good deal in the way of method and a very great deal in the way of aim that all Utopians have in common. Mr. Yeats once suggested that if we put together whatever the great poets have affirmed in their finest moments we should come as near as possible to an authoritative religion. In the same way, one feels that if one tabulated the ideals of the most successful writers of Utopias we should be able to extract, if not a residuum of agreed schemes, at least a common element of aspiration which we might fairly say represented the permanent ideals of the human race respecting the ordering of our life on earth. Really intelligent and altruistic men — and nobody without some intelligence and some altruism would bother to conceive a Utopia — have a tendency to dream the same sort of dreams. To take it on its negative side, no deviser of an ideal state, as far as I am aware, has proposed immense inequalities in the distribution of wealth, crowded and insanitary houses, child labour, wars of aggression, or sweating. There are large numbers of in-

Utopias

dustrious and accurate people in this country and America who are hunting for subjects about which they can write volumes of " research." I wish one of them would write the book I suggest.

Charles II in English Verse

I WAS talking to a man the other day about books that ought to have been written and have not been, when it occurred to me that somebody might publish a very amusing selection of panegyrics written on undeserving persons: say, the less immaculate of the English kings. I once thought of writing a life of Charles II, each chapter of which should be headed by an extract from some contemporary poem about him. The contrast between the character and private and public actions of this monarch and the descriptions of him by literary eulogists would have been illuminating. Gross flattery was the habit of the time. James the First was given, very unfairly as I think, the title of the British Solomon; and the Royal Martyr, who after all had some virtues very highly developed, was written of in terms which would have been extreme if applied to St. Francis of Assisi. But no one, not even his father, received such wholehearted praises as Charles II.

His career as a recipient of them began early. When he was a child Francis Quarles's *Divine Fancies* were dedicated to him. The Dedication was headed: " To the Royal Bud of Majesty and

224

Charles II in English Verse

Cen're of our Hopes and Happiness, Charles," and began: "Illustrious Infant, Give me leave to acknowledge myself thy servant, ere thou knowest thyself my Prince." The hope is held out that the illustrious infant will become " a most incomparable Prince, the firm pillar of our happiness and the future object of the world's wonder." Addressing then the boy's governess, Lady Dorset, Quarles becomes even more rhapsodical:

" Most excellent Lady,
     " You are the Star which stands over the Place where the Babe lies. By whose directions' light, I come from the East to present my Myrrh and Frankincense to the young child. Let not our Royal Joseph nor his princely Mary be afraid; there are no Herods here. We have all seen his Star in the East, and have rejoyced: our loyall hearts are full; for our eyes have seen him, in whom our Posterity shall be blessed.

One could scarcely hope that Quarles's successors would quite live up to that.

Dryden's poem on Charles's return to England is pitched a little lower. It certainly contains lines like

The winds that never moderation knew,
Afraid to blow too much, too faintly blew;

Books in General

Or out of breath with joy would not enlarge
Their straightened lungs . . .

but that is a mere excess of avowed fancy. When
he wrote his *Threnodia Augustalis* on Charles's
death, Dryden decidedly went one better. Perhaps
it was that he had had twenty-five years of Charles's
reign in which to appreciate fully the King's reverend
qualities. He calls him

> *That all-forgiving King*
> *The type of Him above,*
> *That unexhausted spring*
> *Of clemency and love.*

He apostrophizes the Muse of History:

> *Be true, O Clio, to thy hero's name!*
> *But draw him strictly so*
> *That all who view the piece may know;*
> *He needs no trappings of fictitious fame,*
> *The load's too weighty.*

The anguished poet almost blasphemes against
heaven for taking away so peerless a sovereign;
until he remembers that "saints and angels"
had been done out of Charles's company for so
long that their turn might fairly be considered to
have come. And there is the further consolation
that a James has succeeded a Charles:

226

Charles II in English Verse

Our Atlas fell indeed, but Hercules was near;

or, as the Earl of Halifax put it,

James is our Charles in all things else but name.

Which Charles himself at least knew to be untrue.

The Halifax extract comes out of another funeral poem On the Death of His Most Sacred Majesty. " Farewell," he cries,

> *great Charles, monarch of blest renown,*
> *The best good man that ever fill'd a throne.*

He sketches Charles's career. He compares his exile to the banishment of David (an open crib *from Astræ Redux*) and says of England that, when he came back,

> *to his arms she fled*
> *And rested on his shoulders her fair bending head.*

He " Us from our foes and from ourselves did save." Only the almost inevitable comparison to the Almighty can do him justice :

> *In Charles so good a man and King we see*
> *A double image of the deity.*
> *Oh! had he more resembled it! Oh, why*
> *Was he not still more like, and could not die?*

Books in General

What did become of Charles is suggested by "the Lord R" in a poem which appears in *Miscellany Poems:*

Good kings are number'd with Immortal Gods
When hence translated to the best Abodes,
For Princes (truly great) can never die,
They only lay aside Mortality.

After which we are told that the deceased is in Olympus passing the nectar round; an occupation that should have suited him very well.

Perhaps the suggestion will be adopted. Let some publisher with a series of anthologies get somebody to compile The Hundred Most Fulsome Poems in the English Language. It would be a more entertaining book than most. Very few examples, I think, would be drawn from the last hundred years. As respects the monarchs, Great Elizabeth, the Great Jameses, the Great Charleses, Great William, Great Anne, and the Great Georges all got their full share of adulation. The break comes, I think, with George IV; since whose accession we have lost the habit. Any one who should address his sovereign to-day in words like those addressed to Charles II by his subjects (e. g. Great George, the planets tremble at thy nod) would be suspected of pulling the sovereign's leg.

The Most Durable Books

THE question of what books one would take with one for a prolonged sojourn on a desert island is an old one. I thought it had lost its interest for me, as too remote. For I do not propose to live on a desert island; and if ever, by accident, I am cast upon the shore of one, clinging to a solitary plank, it is unlikely that I shall have spent the last hour on shipboard selecting mental food for a highly problematical future as a hermit. But a letter from a distressed man in the trenches revives my interest in the question. He complains that he very rapidly exhausts the books that are sent him; that few of them are much use as permanent companions; and that, as they take up room, he can carry only a small bundle of them about with him. He cannot make up his mind which ones to get and stick to; and he ends by putting the ancient poser to me: "What three" (it is always three) "books would you rather have with you if you had to live on a desert island?" He adds, with somewhat unnecessary bluntness, that he will not believe me if I say that one of them would be the Bible.

I suppose there must be some definition of what a book — what *one* book — is. Otherwise one's first impulse is to demand, as the companions of solitude,

Books in General

the Encyclopædia Britannica, the *Dictionary of National Biography,* and the *Oxford English Dictionary* — say some hundred and twenty volumes in all. With these one could spend a fairly long life in retreat without ever reading the same page twice. One might even read with a definite scheme which would give one the semblance of systematic inquiry united with a happy unexpectedness of route. Suppose, for example, one were to start each day from something one had seen in the morning. A boaconstrictor, for instance. Having twisted its neck and left it for dead — castaways are very powerful fellows — one would go home to the old hut and refer to *Boa in the Encyclopædia.* Having learnt all about its anatomy, progenitiveness, and habitats, one would then refer to the *Oxford Dictionary* for the derivation of its name. Underneath the philological discourse would be quotations from authors who had referred to the beast or to its feathery similitude. The swift advent of the tropic night would find one still immersed in the *D.N.B.* lives of these authors. On a large rock outside one would keep, with a charred stick, a list of the objects already dealt with; once in a way perhaps, for sentiment's sake, one would start from an old word again and revive memories of the Boa Trail. A person of simple tastes, granted the island produced enough goats and not too many constrictors, might well spend in this way a life as contented as Horace's. But to select those three books would be cheating.

The Most Durable Books

One might fairly suggest, in such a connexion, that a book is either (1) any single coherent work by one author, or two in collaboration; or (2) any series of works which either has been, or might reasonably be expected to be, published in a single volume. The edition for island use would not, however, necessarily be a one-volume edition. This rules out these distended works of reference, whilst letting in every single piece of creative literature that exists. There may seem to be an unfair discrimination between author and author, the poets, especially, as a body, being at a great advantage over the novelists; but if novelists will be so verbose they must suffer for it. What, then, would one's three books be?

I can think of a good many books that I have not read and that I hope to enjoy reading. There is *The Life of John Buncle*, there is *Old Mortality*, there is *Hard Times*, there is Tom Paine's *Rights of Man*, there is Hooker's *Ecclesiastical Polity* — and I am imperfectly acquainted with the works of Ben Jonson and Beaumont and Fletcher. (I have also not read *Ordeal by Battle*, and I don't intend to.) But the mere fact that one has not read a work which one knows to be interesting is not enough to qualify it. It would be enough if one were proposing to be marooned for a fortnight or three weeks and then taken off the island by " willing hands "; but the books one wants for a residence of many

years are books one is sufficiently familiar with to be
certain that they will not grow stale at the fifty-fifth
reading.

Well, Gibbon is a large and a very long book.
I have been through it once, and I am pretty sure
I shall do so again. But after that I suspect that
the passages with pencil-marks beside them will satisfy me. I certainly could not, just after finishing
it, recommence it at once, as Lord Randolph
Churchill used to do, or make a practice of dipping
into it daily. Great as it is, it is not sufficiently
varied or sufficiently human. For perpetual reference no general history, I think, would do; one must
have something more of the flavour of everyday
humanity in it. And every mood and every kind
of character must be represented. Though the
books may supplement one another, one finds one's
choice growing at once very narrow. Even Horace
Walpole's *Letters* or Saint-Simon's *Memoirs* would
pall — at any rate on me. Shakespeare will do; but
I cannot personally think of anything which, for me,
would contest the other places with Boswell and
Rabelais, unless it were *Morte d'Arthur.*

There are people, no doubt, who would take *Don
Quixote* or Montaigne. One man I know thinks
that *Tristram Shandy* would go with him. But
Sterne is too short; one would get to know him by
heart in a month or two. *Robinson Crusoe* would

232

The Most Durable Books

have obvious advantages, especially in an illustrated edition — which would provide one with useful models when one was cutting out one's garments. But I think I should take the three I have mentioned — unless, indeed, I approached the matter from quite a different angle. There is a strong case for taking a selection of the more morose and bewildered modern novels — say *La Curée, Le Paradis des Dames,* and *L'Assommoir,* or a judicious selection from Artzybascheff, Mr. Cannan, and Mr. D. H. Lawrence. For these would do a great deal to reconcile one to one's lonely lot. Whenever one was regretting the world of men one would find an everflowing spring of consolation in them. " After all," one would say, after each agued page, " there is a good deal to be said for a desert island."

The Worst Style in the World

THE word "euphuism" is commonly employed: it is also commonly confused with "euphemism." The thing is very properly condemned, and the book that gave it its name is usually condemned with it. But it is probable that John Lyly's *Euphues* has frequently been abused by persons who have never opened it. At any rate, confessions of having read it are few, and have usually proceeded from the small minority who have found merit in the book. It is very interesting, therefore, to see that Messrs. Croll and Clemons have just published, through Routledge, a new edition, fully annotated. A generation unfamiliar with it will have a chance of reassessing it.

The work is in two parts. *Euphues: The Anatomy of Wit* was first published in 1578; *Euphues and his England* in 1580. How immediately popular it was is shown by the fact that (my authority is Mr. Arundell Esdaile's *Bibliography of English Tales and Romances*) four editions of the first part, three of the second, and then at least seventeen editions of both parts together were pub-

234

The Worst Style in the World

lished in fifty-eight years. (His name, incidentally, is spelt on various title-pages Lylly, Lyly, Lylie, Lilie, Lyllie, and Lily: a diversity worthy of " Shakspear.") For a time almost everybody with any pretensions talked and wrote euphuism, very often employing Lyly's fantastic alliterations, antitheses, and superfluous imagery without the content of sense that Lyly always had. Some writers openly ridiculed it. Shakespeare and Jonson made sport with euphuistic characters, and Sidney (who, I think, did not entirely escape the influence) ridiculed this

Talking of beasts, birds, fishes, flies,
Playing with words and idle similes.

But the development of English prose was sensibly changed by it, and its effect may be traced in the prose of Donne, Taylor, and Browne. The book itself, however, like all extravagantly mannered books, had its slump in the end. Early in James I's reign the wider public seems to have turned away from it, and in 1632, E. Blount, the publisher, prefacing an edition of Lyly's plays, referred to him as a forgotten poet whose grave he was digging up. Blount's own language is a terrible example of what Euphuism may come to. He calls his author " a Lilly growing in a Grove of Lawrels ":

" These Papers of his, lay like dead Lawrels in a Churchyard; But I have gathered the scattered

235

Books in General

branches up, and by a Charme (gotten from *Apollo*) made them greene againe, and set up as Epitaphes to his Memory. A sinne it were to suffer these Rare Monuments of wit, to lie covered with Dust, and a shame, such conceipted Comedies, should be acted by none but wormes."

From 1636 to 1868, when the late Professor Arber (a man whose memory has not been sufficiently honoured) published his edition in the " English Reprints," *Euphues* never appeared again, save in two brief eighteenth-century adaptations. For almost a hundred years his names was never mentioned; Lilly the astrologer was much better known. Most eighteenth- and nineteenth-century critics dismissed him as a man who, in Sir Walter Scott's words, deformed his works " by the most unnatural affectation that ever disgraced a printed page." One of the few exceptions was Charles Kingsley, who in *Westward Ho!* attacks Lyly's critics with tremendous enthusiasm:

" I shall only answer by asking, Have they ever read it? For if they have done so, I pity them if they have not found it, in spite of occasional tediousness and pedantry, as brave, righteous, and pious a book as man need look into; and wish for no better proof of the nobleness and virtue of the Elizabethan age than the fact that *Euphues* and the *Arcadia* were the two popular romances of the day."

Turning at this stage, on a sudden impulse, to my

The Worst Style in the World

Encyclopædia, to see whether sense is talked about Lyly there, I find that the article on him is by Mrs. Humphry Ward. Life is full of surprises.

The truth of the matter is that everybody is right, except those who do not trouble to read the book. Kingsley is perfectly correct; it would be difficult to find a book of the time finer in feeling or inspired by higher conceptions of conduct. Lyly is as full of common sense as of refinement; and the fact that he drew much of his discourses on education and religion from other writers does not diminish the impression made by his attitude to life. His narrative does not come to much; most of his space is occupied by harangues, debates, treatises, and letters; his Neapolitan and English love-stories move at a snail's pace. But — his first discussion, by the way, is on heredity and environment which, with startling modernity, he calls Nature and Nurture — he usually argues about things of perennial interest, and always with subtlety, delicacy, and an insight into the human heart. Still, Sir Walter Scott really was not exaggerating the monstrosity — though it is not uniformly monstrous — of his style. It takes some patience to put up with the construction of his sentences and his recurrent bunches of similes in order to follow his argument. On the second page you fall plump into this sentence:

" The freshest colours soonest fade, the keenest Rasor soonest tourneth his edge, the finest cloth is

237

Books in General

soonest eaten with the Moathes, and the Cambricke
sooner stayned than the course Canvas: which appeared well in this Euphues, whose wit beeing like
waxe, apt to receive any impression, and bearing
the head in his own hande, either to use the rayne or
the spurre, disdayning counsaile, leaving his country,
loathing his old acquaintance, thought either by wit
to obteyne some conquest, or by shame to abyde
some conflict, who preferring fancy before friends,
and this present humor, before honour to come, laid
reason in water being too salt for his tast, and followed unbridaled affection, most pleasant for his
tooth."

The mania for balance and alliteration is shown
here, but not the equally characteristic passion for
piling animals and plants, mainly out of Pliny, into
mounds of comparisons. They are most tolerable
when the statements made are least verifiable.
Here are two specimens:

" The filthy Sow when she is sicke, eateth the
Sea-Crab, and is immediately recured: the Torteyse
having tasted the Viper, sucketh Origanum and is
quickly revived: the Beare ready to pine licketh up
the Ants and is recovered: the Dog having surfetted
to procure his vomitte, eateth grasse and findeth
remedy: the Hart beein perced with the dart, run-
neth out of hand to the hearb *Dicbanum,* and is
healed."

238

The Worst Style in the World

" Then good Euphues let the falling out of
friendes be a renewing of affection, that in this we
may resemble the bones of the Lyon, which lying
stil and not moved begin to rot, but being stricken
one against another break out like fire, and wax
greene."

Yet sometimes he will conclude a paragraph of such
abnormalities with a short, humorous, or pathetic
sentence which is most effective; and even sentences
bearing the evident marks of his style sometimes
move one strongly in their context. I may quote
such sentences as Lucilla's two complaints: " But
I would to God Euphues would repair hither that
the sight of him might mitigate some part of my
martyrdome," and the extremely sibilant but musical
" O my Euphues, lyttle dost thou knowe the sodeyn
sorrowe that I susteine for thy sweete sake." What
a really judicious critic would do would be to ridicule
the style and admire the book.

The Reconstruction of Orthography

RECONSTRUCTION is a blessed word, and very comprehensive: but I doubt whether the Government, when it established the Reconstruction Committee, anticipated that it would be asked to consider the problem of Spelling Reform. The Simplified Spelling Society, however, has sent it a memorial urging that " the reform of English spelling is eminently one that merits the practical consideration of the Committee." The signatories include a number of scientific and other professors, scores of teachers, and a tail composed of " men of business, men of letters, editors, etc." The editors do not include any man who edits a London daily or a literary weekly, though the directive minds of the *Lady's Realm* and the *Ardrossan and Saltcoats Herald* are in the movement; and the only " men of letters " are Messrs. William Archer, H. G. Wells, Eden Phillpotts, T. Seccombe (at whom I am surprised), and a few persons who combine authorship with business or with " etc." One did not want this piece of negative evidence to convince one that authors, as a body, will fight Simplifyd Speling to the last mute k. The memorial makes the usual points about saving children's time, facilitating the acquisition of foreign languages, lightening the work of teaching defective children, and assisting aliens who are acquiring our tongue. We are also told that " the demand for a rational spelling may be compared to that for decimalizing our coinage and our weights and measures."

This comparison seems to me very misleading, if by decimalization is meant the introduction of the Continental metric system. For this latter is uniform in various countries, whereas the reform suggested by the Simplified Spelling Society would do nothing to approximate the sound-values of our letters to those of letters in foreign tongues. Cosmopolitan systems have been proposed, very complex and full of odd new letters; but this Society's suggestions, whilst eliminating some difficulties for the foreigner, would leave English just as difficult for a Frenchman to pronounce as French is for an Englishman. Take the phrase (I find it here) " A Ferst Reeder in Simplifyd Speling." A Frenchman would still mispronounce it. If he wished to indicate those sounds in the French way he would write (I am not a phonetician) something like " E Fœust," etc. So the Society had better not pitch its promises too high. This, nevertheless, remains a minor point. The chief considerations undoubtedly are the domestic effects of this piece of Reconstruction.

Books in General

It sounds all very simple and convincing when people say: "Our spoken language has diverged from our written language: let our written language be made the same as our spoken language." But directly you go into the matter you find that the difficulties are enormous. That we have no one spoken language is a commonplace. Our speech varies from fashion to fashion and from locality to locality. "Educated" English at present has an increasing Cockney element in it. The common "cultured" pronunciation of "No," for instance, embodies an "o" sound which is anything but pure. Many rustics, however, still pronounce it with a good broad vowel. Even the spelling reformers do not agree about words. A. J. Ellis thought the "r" at the end of "proper" was still there; Sweet thought it had disappeared. As a matter of fact, it is both there and not there: in some classes and parts it is pronounced, in some it is not. And it is quite possible that it will become universal again.

This gets us on to the question of change in time. The Reformers can be met both ways. If it be argued that phonetic spelling fixes pronunciation, why have we abandoned the old pronunciation of words once phonetically spelt? Shakespeare pronounced the initial "k" in "know" and "knee." We have dropped it out. And we have no guarantee that spelling these words according to our present slack pronunciation would not be followed by an-

The Reconstruction of Orthography

other divergence. The history of the word " sea "
is odd. In the Middle Ages it was spelt " see " and
pronounced " say." In Tudor times the spelling
was altered to " sea " in order to make the spelling
correspond to the sound (the same as that in
" great "). We have reached a pronunciation
which the original spelling would have correctly represented! If it be argued that spelling does not
fix pronunciation, the case for the reform is seriously
weakened. The truth of the matter is that nothing
can fix a pronunciation, but that the written word,
especially in an age of universal literacy, does exer-
cise a pull. And that pull can as well be exercised
by our present spellings as by new ones. I think it
was Titus Oates who went to the scaffold, or somewhere, crying " Lard! Lard! " Had he been a
spelling reformer he would have quite unnecessarily
assimilated the spelling of " lord " with that of the
name of the white stuff they keep in bladders: a
distinct loss to the language. Mr. Murison, in the
Cambridge History of Literature, points out that the
word " kiln " was originally pronounced as spelt;
then for some time the " n " was dropped; then the
old pronunciation returned. The same thing happened to words containing the diphthong " oi."
" Join " and " oil " were, in Middle English, pronounced as they are now. But for centuries men
called them " jine " and " ile," a habit that still
persists amongst many of the most eager supporters
of Spelling Reform. " H's " were dropped whole-

sale and then picked up again. We never know, in fact, whether we shall not return to an old way of speech; and we might as well do that as diverge from an old way of writing.

The great consolation of conservatives in this matter is the length of time during which the enthusiasts have continuously failed to bring about a change. This is the oldest of the Campaigns. It was already old when in 1585 a book was published with this title-page (differently accented) :

" AEsopz Fable'z in true Orto'graphy with Grammar-nótz. Heryuntoo ar al'so joomed the short sentencez of the wyz Cáto imprinted with lyk form and order: both of which Autorz ar transláted out of Latin intoo English. By William Bullokar."

I don't suppose that the Reconstruction Committee will find time to consider this matter. But if they do think of handling it they should realize that they are going to put their hands into a nestful of the largest hornets.

Mr. James Joyce

MR. JAMES JOYCE is a curious phenom-
enon. He first appeared in literary
Dublin about (I suppose) a dozen years
ago: a strangely solitary and self-sufficient and
obviously gifted man. He published a small book
of verse with one or two good lyrics in it; and those
who foresaw a future for him became certain they
were right. He published nothing; but his reputation spread even amongst those who had never read
a line he had written. He disappeared from Ireland
and went to Austria, where he settled. The war
came, and soon afterwards his second book —
Dubliners — was issued and reviewed with a general
deference, after wandering about for years among
publishers who had been fighting shy of it because
of its undoubted unpleasantness and a reference to
Edward VII. Another interval and *A Portrait of
the Artist as a Young Man* began to run serially in
the *Egoist*. "The Egoist, Ltd.," has now published this book, and nobody is surprised to find all
writing London talking about it. Mr. Joyce has
only done what was expected.

Whether this book is supposed to be a novel or
an autobiography I do not know or care. Presum-

ably some characters and episodes are fictitious, or the author would not even have bothered to employ fictitious names. But one is left with the impression that almost all the way one has been listening to sheer undecorated, unintensified truth. Mr. Joyce's title suggests, well enough, his plan. There is no " plot." The subsidiary characters appear and recede, and not one of them is involved throughout in the career of the hero. Stephen Dedalus is born; he goes to school; he goes to college. His struggles are mainly inward: there is nothing unusual in that. He has religious crises: heroes of fiction frequently do. He fights against, succumbs to, and again fights against sexual temptation: we have stories on those lines in hundreds. All the same, we have never had a novel in the least degree resembling this one; whether it is mainly success or mainly failure, it stands by itself.

You recognize its individuality in the very first paragraph. Mr. Joyce tries to put down the vivid and incoherent memories of childhood in a vivid and incoherent way: to show one Stephen Dedalus's memories precisely as one's own memories might appear if one ransacked one's mind. He opens:

" Once upon a time and a very good time it was there was a moocow coming down along the road and the moocow that was down along the road met a nicens little boy named baby tuckoo . . ."

Mr. James Joyce

"His mother had a nicer smell than his father," he proceeds. There is verisimilitude in this; but a critic on the look-out for Mr. Joyce's idiosyncrasies would certainly fasten upon his preoccupation with the olfactory — which sometimes leads him to write things he might as well have left to be guessed at — as one of them. Still, it is a minor characteristic. His major characteristics are his intellectual integrity, his sharp eyes, and his ability to set down precisely what he wants to set down. He is a realist of the first order. You feel that he means to allow no personal prejudice or predilection to distort the record of what he sees. His perceptions may be naturally limited; but his honesty in registering their results is complete. It is even a little too complete. There are some things that we are all familiar with and that ordinary civilized manners (not pharisaism) prevent us from importing into general conversation. Mr. Joyce can never resist a dunghill. He is not, in fact, quite above the pleasure of being shocking. Generally speaking, however, he carries conviction. He is telling the truth about a type and about life as it presents itself to that type.

He is a genuine realist: that is to say, he puts in the exaltations as well as the depressions, the inner life as well as the outer. He is not morosely determined to paint everything drab. Spiritual passions are as powerful to him as physical passions; and as far as his own bias goes it may as well be in

favour of Catholic asceticism as of sensual materialism. For his detachment as author is almost in-
human. If Stephen is himself, then he is a self who
is expelled and impartially scrutinized, without pity
or "allowances," directly Mr. Joyce the artist gets
to work. And of the other characters one may say
that they are always given their due, always drawn
so as to evoke the sympathy they deserve, yet are
never openly granted the sympathy of the author.
He is the outsider, the observer, the faithful selector
of significant traits, moral and physical; his judgments, if he forms them, are concealed. He never
even shows by a quiver of the pen that anything dis-
tresses him.

His prose instrument is a remarkable one. Few
contemporary writers are effective in such diverse
ways; his method varies with the subject-matter and
never fails him. His dialogue (as in the remarkable discussions at home about Barnell and Stephen's
education) is as close to the dialogue of life as anything I have ever come across; though he does not
make the gramophonic mistake of spinning it out as
it is usually spun out in life and in novels that aim
at a faithful reproduction of life and only succeed
in sending one to sleep. And his descriptive and
narrative passages include at one pole sounding periods of classical prose and at the other disjointed
and almost futuristic sentences. The finest sustained pages in the book contain the sermon in which
248

Mr. James Joyce

a dear, simple old priest expounds the unimaginable horrors of hell: the immeasurable solid stench as of a " huge and rolling human fungus," the helplessness of the damned, " not even able to remove from the eye a worm that gnaws it," the fierceness of the fire in which " the blood seethes and boils in the veins, the brains are boiling in the skull, the heart in the breast glowing and bursting, the bowels a red-hot mass of burning pulp, the tender eyes flaming like molten balls." Stephen, after listening to this,

" came down the aisle of the chapel, his legs shaking and the scalp of his head trembling as though it had been touched by ghostly fingers. He passed up the staircase and into the corridor along the walls of which the overcoats and waterproofs hung like gibbeted malefactors, headless and dripping and shapeless."

No wonder. For myself, I had had an idea that this kind of exposition had died with Drexelius; but after I had read it I suddenly and involuntarily thought, " Good Lord, suppose it is all true! " That is a sufficient testimony to the power of Mr. Joyce's writing.

This is not everybody's book. The later portion, consisting largely of rather dull student discussions, is dull; nobody could be inspired by the story, and

Books in General

it had better be neglected by any one who is easily disgusted. Its interest is mainly technical, using the word in its broadest sense; and its greatest appeal, consequently, is made to the practising artist in literature. What Mr. Joyce will do with his powers in the future it is impossible to conjecture. I conceive that he does not know himself: that, indeed, the discovery of a form is the greatest problem in front of him. It is doubtful if he will make a novelist.

Tennessee

LETTERS from strangers can usually be accounted for. But why on earth I, more than any one else, should have received a letter from America asking me to contribute towards the re-establishment of a backwoods library I don't know. This, however, has been my experience, and I trust that I am not endangering the new Anglo-Saxon Entente by relieving my feelings in the following:

LINES

Written on receiving from the Librarian of a College which educates " the mountain youth of Tennessee" a request for " a book" to assist in the re-formation of the Library, which was recently destroyed by fire.

Mine ears have heard your distant moan,
O mountain youth of Tennessee;
Even the bowels of a stone
Would melt to your librarian's plea.
Although we're parted by the ocean,
I'm most distressed about your fire:
Only I haven't any notion
What sort of volume you require.

Books in General

I have a Greene, a Browne, a Gray,
*   A Gilbert White, a William Black,*
Trollope and Lovelace, Swift and Gay,
*   And Hunt and Synge: nor do I lack*
More sober folk for whom out there
*   There may be rather better scope,*
Three worthy men of reverend air,
*   A Donne, a Prior, and a Pope.*

Peacock or Lamb, discreetly taken,
*   Might fill the hungry mountain belly,*
Or Hogg or Suckling, Crabbe or Bacon
*   (Bacon's not Shakespeare, Crabbe is Shelley)*
And if — for this is on the cards —
*   You do not like this mental food,*
I might remit less inward bards:
*   My well-worn Spenser or my Hood.*

Longfellows may be in your line
*   (Littles we know are second-raters),*
Or one might speed across the brine
*   A Mayflower full of Pilgrim Paters.*
Or, then again, you may devote
*   Yourselves to less æsthetic lore,*
Yet if I send you out a Grote*
*   For all I know you'll ask for More.*

O thus proceeds my vacillation:
*   For now the obvious thought returns*

---

* Or, with an appearance of greater generosity, one might return
them the Pound they sent us some years since.

Tennessee

That after such a conflagration
A fitting sequel might be Burns.
And now again I change my mind
And, almost confidently, feel
That since to Beg you are inclined
You might like Borrow, say, or Steele. . . .

Envoi

Yes, Prince, this song shall have an end.
A sudden thought has come to me —
The thing is settled: I shall send
A Tennyson to Tennessee!

But, as a matter of fact, unless I get a special permit
for the export of second-hand books, I shan't be
able to send them even that.

Sir William Watson and Mr. Lloyd George

"REPRESENTATIVES of literature and art" usually appear in the Honours Lists, and they are usually queer representatives. The knighted *littérateur,* as a rule, is either a second-rate man or a man long past his prime. Possibly more men than we know of refuse these knighthoods. For myself I do not see what on earth a really distinguished artist wants with a knighthood, unless he is poor, and thinks that a title would add a guinea or two per thousand to the price of his work. If Sir Samuel Johnson, Sir Charles Dickens, Sir William Blake, Sir Robert Browning, Sir W. Wordsworth, Sir S. Taylor Coleridge, Sir George Meredith stood beside Sir Lewis Morris and Sir W. Robertson Nicoll, Sir Henry Dalziel, and Sir Hedley le Bas (of the Caxton Publishing Company), I do not conceive that those eminent writers would be held in greater honour than they are, or that literature would cut a more important figure in our social life. The one man to whom a knighthood may *usefully* be given is the deserving person who has worked conscientiously for years without adequate recognition and of whose existence the public might — to

Sir Wm. Watson and Mr. Lloyd George

his and its advantage — be officially reminded. As the crown of a famous career a knighthood is absurd.

Sir William Watson has presumably got his knighthood for being one of the most industrious of the war-poets — and a war-poet congenial to the Powers-that-now-Be. Twenty years ago he had a greater reputation than he now has, and wrote several good and many respectable poems. He is still skilful, and can echo effectively the accents of Wordsworth and Milton; but he is certainly not a man of whom one thinks when one is estimating the vital forces in contemporary poetry. A new volume, *The Man who Saw*, has just appeared. The title-poem is about the Prime Minister:

Out of that land where Snowdon night by night
Receives the confidence of lonesome stars,
And where Carnarvon's ruthless battlements
Magnificently oppress the daunted tide,
There comes — no fabled Merlin, son of mist,
And brother to the twilight, but a man
Who in a time terrifically real
Is real as the time; formed for the time;
Not much beholden to the munificent Past,
In mind or spirit, but frankly of this hour;
No faggot of perfections, angel or saint,
Created faultless and intolerable;
No meeting-place of all the heavenlinesses,
But eminently a man to stir and spur
Men, to afflict them with benign alarm,

Books in General

Harass their sluggish and uneager blood,
Till, like himself, they are hungry for the goal;
A man with something of the cragginess
Of his own mountains, something of the force
That goads to their loud leap the mountain streams.

Sir William proceeds to a peroration on

                               the man of Celtic blood,
Whom Powers Unknown, in a divine caprice,
Chose and did make their instrument, wherewith
To save the Saxon; the man all eye and hand,
The man who saw, and grasped, and gripped, and
     held.
Then shall each morrow with its yesterday
Vie, in the honour of nobly honouring him,
Who found us lulled and blindfolded by the verge
Of fathomless perdition and haled us back.
And poets shall dawn in pearl and gold of speech,
Crowning his deed with not less homage, here
On English ground, than yonder whence he rose.

This must certainly be the most eulogistic poem ever
written about a British politician.

There is nothing about Mr. W. M. Hughes,
Lord Milner, Lord Curzon, or Lord Devonport
in the volume; these, perhaps, will be dealt with in
Sir William's next book, which, I do not doubt, will
be ready before long. But Sir Edward Carson gets

Sir Wm. Watson and Mr. Lloyd George

his meed in a sonnet *To the Right Hon. Sir Edward Carson, on leaving Antrim, June* 30, 1916, and another sonnet acclaims Lord Northcliffe — to whom, possibly, there is a delicate allusion in the line quoted above, beginning " Whom Powers." The sonnet is called *The Three Alfreds;* the three being King Alfred, Alfred Lord Tennyson, and Alfred Lord Northcliffe :

Three Alfreds let us honour. Him who drove
His foes before the tempest of his blade
At Ethandune — him first, the all-glorious Shade,
The care-crowned King whose host with Guthrum
    strove.
Next — though a thousand years asunder clove
These twain — a lord of realms serenely swayed;
Victoria's golden warbler, him who made
Verse such as Virgil for Augustus wove.
Last — neither king nor bard, but just a man
Who, in the very whirlwind of our woe,
From midnight till the laggard dawn began,
Cried ceaseless, " Give us shells — more shells," and
    so
Saved England; saved her not less truly than
Her hero of heroes saved her long ago.

It is a pity that there could not have been added some reference to Lord Northcliffe's conviction that nobody in his senses ever dreamed of using shrapnel against wire. Had the shells passage been expanded it might have been less cacophonous. As it stands, it gives rise to the suspicious illusion that the sibilant cry was uttered by Mr. (or is it Sir?) Wilkie Bard. But no; it was " neither King nor Bard."

Stranded

"NO," I thought, "I won't take any books with me. I want a rest. I shall swim. I shall catch fish. There is sure to be a billiard-room in that pub., and pretty certain to be a few people who play bridge. The overtaxed brain must be allowed relaxation. So good-bye, Plato; good-bye, Spinoza; good-bye, Samuel Rawson Gardiner; good-bye, Freud. I won't take any of you."

I had been in the place twenty-four hours, and had plumbed the depths of my neighbours' incapacity to play any games of skill or chance (except possibly — I did not ask this — loo and vingt-et-un), when, sauntering down the main, and indeed the only, street, I caught sight of the words, "Grocer, Chemist, Tobacconist, Draper, and Circulating Library." It would be ungracious, I felt, to let such versatility go unrecognized. Besides, one might as well take a novel or two out with one in the boat. It might make the intervals between the bites seem a little shorter. So in I went.

A young girl with a pigtail escorted me past the Quaker Oats and the Gold Flakes, under a little

Books in General

low doorway and into a back room. "A shilling deposit, and twopence on each book," she said; and left me to the shelves. There were books there all right: about two thousand of them, reaching from floor to ceiling on both sides. There was no sort of order, alphabetical or otherwise, so it was no good expecting to find a particular author right off. The only thing for it was beginning somewhere and going steadily along the rows.

B. M. Croker: yes, I think I read a great many of hers in my youth. They were about penniless young ladies going to India and getting married. It is no good tackling this one. *The Gateless Barrier,* by Lucas Malet; that was about spiritualism, and pretty average tosh it was; I shall probably come to *Sir Richard Calmady* presently, but I shall give him a miss too. *The Iron Pirate:* I liked that rather, but it would be a pity not to like it so much now. I feel the same about *Saracinesca, The Witch of Prague,* and *In the Palace of the King,* which are all in a lump together where some late devotee has replaced them. Marion Crawford, upon whose every word my childhood hung, I dare not attempt you again; even *A Cigarette Maker's Romance* and the chronicle of *Mr. Isaacs* (who enjoyed Kant and deluded me, for a time, into the belief that I should like him too) will be more dear to the memory if they are not restored to sight. *Count Hannibal:* that was the man who either massacred somebody

Stranded

or escaped massacre on St. Bartholomew's Day.
He had a great square jaw and eyes that made you
jump; and women cowered and obeyed when he
emitted a short, sharp oath or looked like emitting
one. Wiliam Black I never liked at any time, so
nothing by him need detain me. *Flames?* No.
Dodo? Oh dear, no. *Ships that pass in the
Night?* No. There was edelweiss in it, and an
old man who was otherworldly and read nothing but
Gibbon. Queen Victoria thought highly of it, but
I don't want to read it again. Nor *Red Pottage*
either. The husband and the other man (I think)
had a duel. They drew straws, and the man with
the shortest straw had to kill himself. What the
lady thought about it I don't remember. But one of
them was a Lord, New Zealand came in somewhere, and at suitable places in the conversation a
moth would flutter or a kingfisher flash by. It is by
touches like these that one can distinguish really
imaginative literature, but I am not tempted.

It is not reasonable to expect a man at this date
to return to *A Yellow Aster,* or *Moths* by Ouida.
As for *The Silence of Dean Maitland,* the predica-
ment of that respected ecclesiastic with the undis-
closed sin on his conscience is still fresh in my mind,
and I still remember how my elders, when it first
came out, debated whether such a book ought to be
written, and whether Maxwell Gray was a man or
a woman. Of *The Sorrows of Satan* I recall little

261

of the plot, except that the Devil was a gentleman. I think that the first sentences were: " Do you know what it is to be poor? Not with that — poverty that — on ten thousand a year, but with that grinding poverty that," etc. How many years ago is it since that immortal paragraph, reproduced in facsimile from the author's own script, appeared in the *Strand Magazine,* with pictures of the great novelist in divers postures? It would be Ethel M. Dell now, I suppose; but they don't seem to keep Miss Dell's works in this Circulating Library, of which the circulation seems to have stopped many, many, many years since. They keep instead Frankfort Moore and G. B. Burgin.

Anthony Hope now. Here is *The Intrusions of Peggy.* There was a grizzled inventor who lived in the Temple, and he had a daughter (?) who shone like a sunbeam amidst the dusty shades of the law. Anthony Hope, who was very nearly a first-rate writer, must have put it better than that; but I'm sure that that is what it was about. Seton Merriman now. This is better. But will or will not a reperusal of *The Vultures* and *Roden's Corner* diminish the respect that still survives in me for him? He gave me immense pleasure at one time; can I risk it? I don't know.

With meditations like the above I roamed up and down before the frayed and wrinkled backs of

Stranded

these veterans, fascinated by so systematic a recovery of the familiar. Then I remembered that the sun was shining in a blue sky, only slightly fleeced with cloud; that the salt wind blowing shoreward was driving broken sunlight over the waves; that there were as good fish in the sea as ever came out of it; and that I must really take care of my health. Catching sight of *She* and *Many Cargoes,* which I have read at least ten times apiece, but am always good for again, I detached them from their faded companions and took them into the front shop, meditating upon the astonishing sluggishness of this shop, where even Mrs. Barclay had not yet penetrated and Garvice was a cloudy speculation in the far future.

I paid my one-and-fourpence and stepped out on to the cobblestones. As I passed into the sun, it occurred to me that it was not surprising that even the minor works in the library were like old friends. For — and things like these do strangely remain known, yet for a time, unrelated — I spent a summer in this village fifteen years ago.

Mr. Ralph Hodgson

MR. RALPH HODGSON is a poet who has still not quite got his due. He has just collected into one volume (*Poems*), with a few others, the verses published in a series of " Flying Fame Booklets " with Mr. Lovat Fraser's charming and ingenious cuts. Ten years' work goes into seventy pages, so that a charge of over-production is scarcely possible. In the circumstances Mr. Hodgson might have included one or two poems, *The Last Blackbird,* for example, from his earlier book. That book as a whole, however, was not comparable with this, which contains *The Bull,* indubitably one of the finest poems of our generation, *The Song of Honour,* which is almost as good, and many charming lighter lyrics. *Eve,* particularly, is a feat. Mr. Hodgson makes a delicate tripping song out of the Fall of Man; he pictures Eve, " that orchard sprite,"

> *Wondering, listening,*
> *Listening, wondering,*
> *Eve with a berry*
> *Half-way to her lips,*

and the serpent, a graceful beast,

264

Mr. Ralph Hodgson

Tumbling in twenty rings
Into the grass.

The whole story trips like that.

> *" Eva! " Each syllable*
> *Light as a flower fell,*
> *" Eva! " he whispered the*
> *Wondering maid,*
> *Soft as a bubble sung*
> *Out of a linnet's lung,*
> *Soft and most silverly*
> *" Eva! " he said.*

But — and this is the achievement — one is not left with a sense of inadequacy and triviality. For the feeling throughout is sincere, and the nature of the calamity is conveyed as clearly by Mr. Hodgson, who makes the small birds chatter with sorrow and indignation when Eve falls, as it would have been by another man with all the paraphernalia of darkening heavens, thunderous voices, and long Latin words.

But this poem is not on the same plane as *The Bull* and *The Song of Honour*. No writer has ever entered more completely into the feelings of an animal than does Mr. Hodgson as, in a setting of tropical forest and swamp, he shows the defeated, expelled, and dying leader of the herd remembering

265

Books in General

his calfhood, and his early fights, and his prowess
and his final fall, whilst the obscene birds circle
round overhead waiting for his death. *The Song
of Honour,* an attempt to echo the Hymn of Praise
sung by all things to their Maker, is, in the nature
of things, more disjointed and impressionistic, less
exact and well-shaped. It owes as much as any
poem can decently owe to another to Christopher
Smart's *Song to David.* But the strength of feeling
never fails, and parts of the breathless pæan are
very beautiful.

> *The music of a lion strong*
> *That shakes a hill a whole night long,*
> *A hill as loud as he,*
> *The twitter of a mouse among*
> *Melodious greenery,*
> *The ruby's and the rainbow's song,*
> *The nightingale's — all three,*
> *The song of life that wells and flows*
> *From every leopard, lark and rose*
> *And everything that gleams or goes*
> *Lack-lustre in the sea.*
>
>   .   .   .   .   .
>
> *I heard it all, I heard the whole*
> *Harmonious hymn of being roll*
> *Up through the chapel of my soul*
> *And at the altar die,*
> *And in the awful quiet then*
> *Myself I heard, Amen, Amen,*

Mr. Ralph Hodgson

Amen I heard me cry!
I heard it all and then although
I caught my flying senses, Oh,
A dizzy man was I!
I stood and stared; the sky was lit,
The sky was stars all over it,
I stood, I knew not why,
Without a wish, without a will,
I stood upon that silent hill
And stared into the sky until
My eyes were blind with stars and still
I stared into the sky.

Those are two of the last stanzas, and even standing alone, I think, give something of the quality of the poem. They certainly are characteristic in the simplicity of their language.

Double Misprints

I TAKE the following paragraph from the *Connersville (Ind.) Herald:*

" The Guest Day meeting of the literary club will be held at the home of Mrs. L. A. Frazer to-morrow afternoon. Mrs. De Morgan Jones, of Indianapolis, will lecture on " William Butler Meats and the Garlic Revival."

I think the Lady of Shalott should have been brought in. Double misprints are rare, but I remember another which also was perpetrated in America but which has not quite so convincing an air of sheer accident as this one. A Colonel, who had fought in the Civil War, was described in his local paper as " a battle-scared veteran." This imputation on his courage brought him to the office with a big stick and a demand that the paragraph should be reprinted with the offensive remark corrected. It was: but another misprint crept in and the word appeared as " bottle-scarred." Every one who has dealings with the Press occasionally corrects, amid the mass of quite meaningless " literals," a misprint that really makes some sort of sense.

268

Double Misprints

I myself in the last few months have had to emend
printers' references to Mr. Hotairio Bottomley and
Mr. Edmund Goose. The former one felt tempted
to leave uncorrected, the derangement of letters being so extremely apt.

The History of Earl Pumbles

THE late Earl (Eorl?) Pumbles was of lowly birth. He was born in the thorp of Stoke Parva in 1850, the son of a penniless timber-wright. Outdriven from his first school, he became a fighting-man. He was a dreadless and fearnought wight, and was once left for dead on the field, bleeding at every sweat-hole. The saw-bones brought him through. Coming back to England he saw the haplihood of making a gold-hoard in the soap-trade. He set up a business with the gold of others; got rid of his yoke-mates by sundry under-slinkings, and soon became amazingly wealthy. An earldom followed; though it is markworthy that on the morning after its bestowal a great songsmith wrote to the *Daily Score* to say: 'The Gusher of Fair-Name is befouled.' In 1910 Lord Pumbles went as sendling to the King of Siam, with a bode-word from our King. In the back-end of the next year his health gave out; he became bit-wise worse; and he died last night of belly-ache. Lord Pumbles was often to be seen at Sir Henry Wood's Out-Road Glee-Motes at Queen's Hall, but he was almost a comeling at the House of Lords. He was cunning in Kin-lore, and in his fair wonestead at Pumbles

The History of Earl Pumbles

wrote a great book on the stem-tree of his kin. By ill hap he was an eat-all and rather soaksome. He will be buried on Wednesday in the bone-yard at Pumbles, in which lich-rest his wife already lies. The earldom goes, by out-of-the-way odd-come-short, to his daughter."

This little biography may have puzzled those who have got thus far. They may have thought it absurd. I compiled it with the help of " C. L. D.'s " *Word-Book of the English Tongue,* just published by Routledge. " C. L. D." (the initials are, I observe, those of the author of *Alice in Wonderland*) is one of those enthusiasts who long " to shake off the Norman yoke " which lies so heavy on our speech. He follows, that is to say, in the footsteps of the late Rev. William Barnes (of Dorset), who asked his countrymen to call a perambulator a " child-wain " and an omnibus a " folk-wain." " What many speakers and writers," he remarks, " even to-day, call English, is no English at all but sheer French. Nevertheless, there are many who feel not a little ashamed of the needless loan-words in which their speech is clothed, and of the borrowed feathers in which they strut. Over and over again it has been said, and most truly, that for liveliness and strength, manliness and fulness of meaning, the olden English Tongue were hard to beat." " In this little Word-Book, therefore," he says:

Books in General

" after having chosen a few thousand stock loan-words, I have striven to set by the side of each, not indeed ' synonyms,' but other good English words, which may stand in their stead."

Which is certainly (or, I think I should say, " ywis " or " in good sooth ") a pure English sentence.

One primary fault " C. L. D." avoids almost entirely. He does not (as he might have done had he cared to take all the astonishing Latin words from Johnson's Word-Book) load the dice by including in his list of " loan-words " words which we hardly ever use. There are a few. Only a scientist would say " acephalous " when he meant " headless "; and the general public does not need to be warned to say " grind," " bristly," " stalkless," and " barefooted," instead of " comminute," " aristate," " acaulescent," and " discalced." It would never dream of saying acaulescent. Where our author errs is where he would inevitably err: in suggesting to us (1) Saxon words which we simply won't use, and (2) Saxon words which do not take the place of the Latin words of which he disapproves. Take, for instance, as an instance of the latter category, this very word " disapprove." All he can give us is a list of " strong " words beginning with " hiss " and " hoot," none of which gets the exact shade of meaning required. Similarly with

272

The History of Earl Pumbles

" decry," for which his suggestions are " boo " and
" hoot." In suggesting " clean," " flat," etc., for
" absolute " he is merely booing and hooting the
slang use of that word, but he has not found a
Saxon equivalent for the real " absolute." For
" complimentary " he gives " smooth-spoken "; but
how would, say, the Archbishop of Canterbury like
to get a letter of thanks beginning: " My dear
Archbishop,— Many thanks for your very smooth-
spoken remarks "? For " uncomfortable " he can
only suggest writhing "— as though we could say
that we had spent a fortnight in a most writhing
hotel; and for " temporalities " he has nothing but
" loaves and fishes "— which is simply offensive.
If one began using words like these promiscuously,
one would simply (here I consult the *Word-Book*
again) be asking for misluck.

To turn to the other lot, it is altogether too late
to ask us to say " rede-craft " for " logic "; " back-
jaw " for " retort "; " handmaid " for " servant ";
" outganger " for " emigrant "; " wanhope " (a
most beautiful word, I admit) for " despair ";
" scald " or " songsmith " for " poet "; " hight "
or " yclept " for " denominated "; " uplooking "
for " aspiring "; " fourwinkled " for " quadrangu-
lar "; and, above all, to replace " depilatory " by
" hair-bane." " Ereold " and " foreold " for
" ancient " are no longer possible; and the man who

273

should say that the King was crowned and be-smeared in Westminster Abbey would be quite un-able to persuade people that he wasn't merely a rather coarse satirist. In cases where both terms are alive, the Latin is often more convenient — be-cause shorter — than the Saxon. If we always used " breach of wedlock " instead of " adultery," many modern novels, and most Sunday newspapers, would use up twice as much paper and ink. (There was once a half-way word: the mediæval heralds used to say that the leopard was " begotten in spouse-breach between the lion and the pard.") In pro-posing " hand-grip " for portmanteau, our word-loresman is doing an audacious thing: adopting a bit of modern American — though, as often as not, the term is shortened, across the water, to " grip " *tout court.*

There remain, of course, a very large number of words for which " C. L. D." does provide genuine living synonyms which, in many cases, are stronger and terser than the originals. Even here, of course, there are occasional difficulties; we have, at any rate in print, thrown over " C. L. D.'s " favourites " belly-ache " and " gripes " in favour of " colic " simply because they *are* what is called " good sturdy Saxon," altogether too apt and sturdy. As for his proposal of " ropes " and " manifolds " for " intes-tines," all I can say is that I much prefer here to remain under the Norman yoke. At the same time, too much Latinity is a nuisance and a danger to the

The History of Earl Pumbles

vividness of our tongue; and, whilst refraining from following " C. L. D." to his thorps or Barnes to his folk-wain, I think I shall sometimes find the *Word-Book* useful.

On Destroying Books

"IT says in the paper" that over two million volumes have been presented to the troops by the public. It would be interesting to inspect them. Most of them, no doubt, are quite ordinary and suitable; but it was publicly stated the other day that some people were sending the oddest things, such as magazines twenty years old, guides to the Lake District, Bradshaws, and back numbers of *Whitaker's Almanack*. In some cases, one imagines, such indigestibles get into the parcels by accident; but it is likely that there are those who jump at the opportunity of getting rid of books they don't want. Why have kept them if they don't want them? But most people, especially non-bookish people, are very reluctant to throw away anything that looks like a book. In the most illiterate houses that one knows every worthless or ephemeral volume that is bought finds its way to a shelf and stays there. In reality it is not merely absurd to keep rubbish merely because it is printed: it is positively a public duty to destroy it. Destruction not merely makes more room for new books and saves one's heirs the trouble of sorting out the rubbish or storing it: it may also prevent posterity from making a fool of itself. We

On Destroying Books

may be sure that if we do not burn, sink, or blast all
the superseded editions of Bradshaw, two hundred
years hence some collector will be specializing in old
railway time-tables, gathering, at immense cost, a
complete series, and ultimately leaving his " treasures " (as the Press will call them) to a Public Institution.

But it is not always easy to destroy books. They
may not have as many lives as a cat, but they certainly die hard; and it is sometimes difficult to find
a scaffold for them. This difficulty once brought
me almost within the Shadow of the Rope. I was
living in a small and (as Shakespeare would say)
heaven-kissing flat in Chelsea, and books of inferior
minor verse gradually accumulated there until at last
I was faced with the alternative of either evicting
the books or else leaving them in sole, undisturbed
tenancy and taking rooms elsewhere for myself.
Now, no one would have bought these books. I
therefore had to throw them away or wipe them
off the map altogether. But how? There were
scores of them. I had no kitchen range, and I could
not toast them on the gas-cooker or consume them
leaf by leaf in my small study fire — for it is almost
as hopeless to try to burn a book without opening it
as to try to burn a piece of granite. I had no dust-
bin; my debris went down a kind of flue behind the
staircase, with small trap-doors opening to the land-
ings. The difficulty with this was that the larger

277

books might choke it; the authorities, in fact, had labelled it " Dust and Ashes Only "; and in any case I did not want to leave the books intact, and some dustman's unfortunate family to get a false idea of English poetry from them. So in the end I determined to do to them what so many people do to the kittens: tie them up and consign them to the river. I improvised a sack, stuffed the books into it, put it over my shoulder, and went down the stairs into the darkness.

It was nearly midnight as I stepped into the street. There was a cold nip in the air; the sky was full of stars; and the greenish-yellow lamps threw long gleams across the smooth, hard road. Few people were about; under the trees at the corner a Guardsman was bidding a robust good night to his girl, and here and there rang out the steps of solitary travellers making their way home across the bridge to Battersea. I turned up my overcoat collar, settled my sack comfortably across my shoulders, and strode off towards the little square glow of the coffee-stall which marked the near end of the bridge, whose sweeping iron girders were just visible against the dark sky behind. A few doors down I passed a policeman who was flashing his lantern on the catches of basement windows. He turned. I fancied he looked suspicious, and I trembled slightly. The thought occurred to me: " Perhaps he suspects

On Destroying Books

I have swag in this sack." I was not seriously disturbed, as I knew that I could bear investigation, and that nobody would be suspected of having stolen such goods (though they *were* all first editions) as I was carrying. Nevertheless I could not help the slight unease which comes to all who are eyed suspiciously by the police, and to all who are detected in any deliberately furtive act, however harmless. He acquitted me, apparently; and, with a step that, making an effort, I prevented from growing more rapid, I walked on until I reached the Embankment.

It was then that all the implications of my act revealed themselves. I leaned against the parapet and looked down into the faintly luminous swirls of the river. Suddenly I heard a step near me; quite automatically I sprang back from the wall and began walking on with, I fervently hoped, an air of rumination and unconcern. The pedestrian came by me without looking at me. It was a tramp, who had other things to think about; and, calling myself an ass, I stopped again. " Now's for it," I thought; but just as I was preparing to cast my books upon the waters I heard another step — a slow and measured one. The next thought came like a blaze of terrible blue lightning across my brain: " What about the splash? " A man leaning at midnight over the Embankment wall: a sudden fling of his arms: a great splash in the water. Surely, and not without reason, whoever was within sight and hearing (and

279

there always seemed to be some one near) would at once rush at me and seize me. In all probability they would think it was a baby. What on earth would be the good of telling a London constable that I had come out into the cold and stolen down alone to the river to get rid of a pack of poetry? I could almost hear his gruff, sneering laugh: " You tell that to the Marines, my son! "

So for I do not know how long I strayed up and down, increasingly fearful of being watched, summoning up my courage to take the plunge and quailing from it at the last moment. At last I did it. In the middle of Chelsea Bridge there are projecting circular bays with seats in them. In an agony of decision I left the Embankment and hastened straight for the first of these. When I reached it I knelt on the seat. Looking over, I hesitated again. But I had reached the turning-point. " What! " I thought savagely, " under the resolute mask that you show your friends is there really a shrinking and contemptible coward? If you fail now, you must never hold your head up again. Anyhow, what if you *are* hanged for it? Good God! you worm, better men than you have gone to the gallows! " With the courage of despair I took a heave. The sack dropped sheer. A vast splash. Then silence fell again. No one came. I turned home; and as I walked I thought a little sadly of all those books falling into that cold torrent, settling slowly down

On Destroying Books

through the pitchy dark, and subsiding at last on the ooze of the bottom, there to lie forlorn and forgotten whilst the unconscious world of men went on.

Horrible bad books, poor innocent books, you are lying there still; covered, perhaps, with mud by this time, with only a stray rag of your sacking sticking out of the slime into the opaque brown tides. Odes to Diana, Sonnets to Ethel, Dramas on the Love of Lancelot, Stanzas on a First Glimpse of Venice, you lie there in a living death, and your fate is perhaps worse than you deserved. I was harsh with you. I am sorry I did it. But even if I had kept you, I will certainly say this: I should not have sent you to the soldiers.

THE END